WHO DOES YOUR GARDEN GROW?

Alex Pankhurst

WHO DOES
YOUR GARDEN GROW?

Earl's Eye Publishing

For my parents

First published in 1992
by Earl's Eye Publishing
Lamb Corner, Dedham
Colchester CO7 6EE, England

ISBN 0 9518133 0 7

A CIP catalogue record for this book is available
from the British Library

Photoset by Rowland Phototypesetting Ltd
Bury St Edmunds, Suffolk
Printed in Great Britain by
Simmons Printers Ltd
Chelmsford, Essex

CONTENTS

ACKNOWLEDGEMENTS

So many kind people gave help with this book—they cannot all be formally acknowledged here, but I am very aware of my debt.

In particular my thanks are due to Graham Thomas, Arthur Hellyer, Chris Brickell, Frances Perry, Alan Bloom, Joe Elliott, Anthony Huxley, Jack Gingell, Arthur Heard and Pat Edwards; to officers of the National Council for the Conservation of Plants and Gardens, and the holders of various National Collections; as well as to so many relatives and friends of 'Plant People'. All gave time, and responded patiently to my probings for information.

I should also like to thank Natalie Finch, Pat and Doug Taylor, Jean Sambrook, Richard Bird and Jane Sterndale-Bennett for all their help and encouragement; Lorna Schärer and Tina Batey for local research; Janet Dampney and Joan Lewis for the loan of books; and Stephen Taffler, for sparking off the idea in the first place.

I am much indebted to my non-gardening father, who diligently read and commented on every page as it was written; to Lewis Hart who kindly scrutinised the manuscript for botanical inexactitudes; and to Dr Brent Elliott and his staff at the Royal Horticultural Society's Lindley Library, without whose humbling knowledge, help and efficiency this book could never have been written.

Lastly I have to thank my family, who over the last three years have had to put up with even worse meals than usual. That was asking a lot.

INTRODUCTION

'I want a Horticultural Who's Who. The Who's Who should not only tell who *is* who in gardening, but who *was* who and *what* who was and *when*. I want to know who Mrs Sinkins was, Dorothy Perkins, Maggie Mott and Linda Pope. One would like to know something of the folk after whom were named plants which in our own time have taken the world by storm, or which took it by storm fifty or a hundred years ago and still hold their own as first class varieties.' So wrote nurseryman and gardening journalist Clarence Elliott in 1930.

His plea went unanswered, and some sixty years later there was still nothing to tell enquiring gardeners who their plants commemorated. Now I know why. Seeking the information is as frustrating as sowing trillium seed.

Perhaps it is not surprising. Big nurseries produced hundreds of plants, often naming them after customers, family members, or the donor of the original plant. Nurserymen could not be expected to explain in their catalogues who these people were. Nor could anyone forecast which of the multitude of novelties would become 'classics', held in esteem and affection half a century or more later.

The story differs where plants were named after famous gardens or gardeners. The contemporary gardening world would have known where they originated, just as present day gardeners need no explanation when named plants come from Bressingham, Beth Chatto or Wisley. Origins that are widely known are seldom considered worth recording, thus what is common knowledge to one generation is often lost to the next.

Three years' research have given me a fascinating glimpse of the changing, yet seemingly timeless, gardening scene over the last 150 years. The day of rich enthusiasts with lavish and perfectly-kept private gardens may have gone, but to read their complaints about slugs and rabbits, plants determined to die, the unpredictable British climate, and botanists who *keep* altering the names, is to feel that gardening never really changes. And it is a thing of balance. Today we may not have cheap labour but, to compensate, our predecessors have left us a legacy of wonderful plants.

For garden plants do not simply happen. Foreign plants have all been introduced by somebody, many collectors devoting their lives to the specie plants we take for granted today. Cultivars may likewise represent a gardening lifetime—years of patient breeding, or the cherishing of a special plant which saved it from extinction.

Even cultivars which originated as chance seedlings or mutations, owe their continued existence to someone's observant eye.

Ah, but what is a cultivar? A botanist could give a long and precise definition, while I am a mere gardener. This book includes other named plants, but in my understanding a cultivar is a plant with distinctive characteristics, found nowhere in the wild, i.e. of garden origin. The name comes from the words 'cultivated variety', and there is a nice story, probably apocryphal, about the gardener who coined the term immediately regretting it. Too late, the word had escaped.

I have tried hard to be accurate, but delving for information about people who have become famous as plants is a daunting task. Frequent name changing by the botanists complicates research, and even apparently reputable sources can be quite simply, wrong. Whenever possible, therefore, I have gone back to the writings of the people concerned, or traced their friends and relatives.

If the plant name that most intrigues you gets no mention, I can only apologise for the disappointment. Like as not it was a nineteenth century French rose, and trying to glean information on their namesakes proved about as rewarding as struggling to grow double primroses in my parched and gravelly garden. French nurseries produced thousands of roses, of which only a handful are now widely grown, and names like 'Jamain' and 'Carrière', which have such a romantic ring, are not the uncommon surnames they sound to us. A few yielded sufficient information to be included, but regretfully, the rest must be left to a masochistic French gardener or English ex-patriot.

Leaving aside nineteenth century roses, no book of this kind can ever be comprehensive, given the thousands of cultivars, but then the majority actually disappear over the years. Plants are superseded, lose vigour, or are simply not grown by enough people to ensure their continuance. Of the thousands of named plants listed by the Royal Horticultural Society at the turn of the century, very few still exist. With occasional exceptions, therefore, most modern cultivars have been excluded, since only time will sort out the ones with real quality and staying power.

The plants included were chosen either because they are very widely grown; commemorate great gardens or gardeners; or have particularly intriguing names. (There are obvious omissions—so much has been written by and about Gertrude Jekyll and Margery

Fish and their plants and gardens, that I have not included them here.)

Since it is irritating to read about a desirable plant which you cannot go out and buy, another criterion was that the plants should still be commercially available, and here The Plant Finder was my guide. Unfortunately what might have been available when I re-searched, may not be listed today. Conversely some plants now appear in The Plant Finder which seemed not to be available before. Such is Life.

Hardy plants make up the majority covered, this being the area of gardening I know most about—if one writes from complete ignorance it tends to show. Inevitably the selection is arbitrary and subjective, but I hope the stories behind these plants will interest a broad range of gardeners, and perhaps stimulate the purchase of new plants, as it has with me.

In my own small garden, amongst many others *Schizostylis* 'Viscountess Byng' now flowers charmingly (in a good year), *Cheiranthus* 'Harpur Crewe' welcomes visitors to the front door, *Phlox* 'Norah Leigh' has a choice spot, *Sedums* 'Bertram Anderson' and 'Vera Jameson' give excellent value, and *Tropaeolum tuberosum* 'Ken Aslet' hides the bathroom downpipes. The plot may not be much to look at, but it now grows a satisfying crop of gardeners.

Alex Pankhurst
Dedham, Essex
1992

EMPRESS JOSEPHINE
1763–1814

Rose 'Empress Josephine'
Rose 'Souvenir de la Malmaison'

Marie Josephine Rose Tascher de la Pagerie was born in 1763 on the French West Indian island of Martinique. She was a creole, her father a naval officer, who subsequently returned to France taking his vivacious, sixteen-year-old daughter with him. There she soon married the Vicomte de Beauharnais, son of the Governor of Martinique, but fifteen years later he was executed. So it was an attractive widow with two children who was introduced to Napoleon Bonaparte and became his wife.

The Chateau de la Malmaison outside Paris was a seventeenth century house badly in need of repair, but it was just what Josephine wanted for her country home. She was a keen gardener, and in due course the newly-landscaped gardens contained a large number of rare and exotic plants. Her first love, however, was roses.

Josephine was determined to collect together all the roses then known, and had plants sent to her from far and wide. The blockading English navy even had orders to allow safe passage for one ship, aboard which was an English nurseryman named Kennedy, delivering an order for Malmaison. Napoleon sent examples back from wherever he was campaigning, and eventually the collection grew to some 200 different roses. The Empress had succeeded in her ambition. She took pleasure in giving names to those that apparently had none, and it is to her that we owe the imaginitively named 'Cuisse de Nymph Émue'—literally translated 'Thigh of an Aroused Nymph', or more modestly 'Maiden's Blush'.

Unable to give Napoleon an heir, Josephine was divorced by him in 1810, and devoted herself entirely to Malmaison until she became ill and died in 1814. She had however commissioned the famous botanical artist Pierre-Joseph Redouté to make a record of her roses. Thus despite the garden at Malmaison becoming overgrown, and finally destroyed by the Prussian army, the majority of her roses live on in his wonderful paintings. She had also made her favourite flower fashionable, and French nurserymen began to lead the world in rose breeding.

It is perhaps surprising that only two roses now commemorate Josephine and her garden. The delicately flesh-pink Bourbon rose 'Souvenir de la Malmaison' was bred some thirty years after her death, and grown at Malmaison where rosarians were trying to re-establish the garden. It had no official name, but the Grand Duke of Russia visited one day and was very taken with it. He obtained a plant for the Imperial Garden and called it 'Souvenir de la Malmaison'. There is both a bush and a climbing form, and in good summers it produces magnificent quartered blooms up to five inches across, flowering a second time in September.

The rose called 'Empress Josephine' is now thought rightfully to be *Rosa francofurtana*, known in gardens for well over a hundred years before its namesake was born. The heavily-veined flowers of this Gallica rose are dark pink, and semi-double. The story goes that it was brought to this country in the nineteenth century by French emigrés. If they called it 'Empress Josephine', perhaps it was a particular favourite of the Empress who loved roses.

MADAME HARDY

Rose 'Madame Hardy'

Madame Hardy was the wife of a man widely respected in the French horticultural world of the mid-nineteenth century. Monsieur Hardy was Superintendent of the Luxembourg Gardens in Paris, an acknowledged expert on the management of fruit trees, fittingly commemorated by a pear still grown today, 'Beurré Hardy'.

In the days when all great houses relied on quantities of first class fruit and vegetables from their kitchen gardens, there was particular interest in that branch of horticulture. The Luxembourg Gardens devoted a whole area to demonstrating the different ways of growing fruit trees, and besides being responsible for the day to day running of the large gardens, Monsieur Hardy gave talks.

An English visitor in 1847 reported hastening to the gardens in March to hear a lecture on pruning, given in the open at eight in the morning. 'Monsieur Hardy delivers two lectures every week, free to the public,', he reported, 'on pruning, grafting, planting and everything connected with the management of fruit trees, finishing the course in the end of April. He has generally 300 to 400 hearers, among whom are the young men employed in the Luxembourg Gardens and other establishments. But the greater number of those who attend are amateurs.' In the afternoon Hardy would lecture again, this time 'to gentlemen wishing to obtain a knowledge of the management of fruit trees', and they paid three francs each for the privilege.

There was great enthusiasm in nineteenth century France for breeding new roses, and perhaps Monsieur Hardy indulged in it as a hobby. At any rate in 1832 he produced a new rose, named after his wife. Probably the result of crossing a Damask rose with a Centifolia, his creation was a strong-growing shrub rose, with handsome foliage and double, sweetly-scented flowers borne in clusters. Each flower began creamy white, becoming pure white as it opened fully, revealing a small green button in the centre.

Rose growing became so popular that by 1885 there were over six thousand varieties of rose available for the general public to buy. That year a French rose journal recommended 'Madame Hardy' as one of the best twenty-six varieties available—a mark of quality, amidst so much competition. It has remained popular, indeed has been described as 'the most beautiful white rose in existence.'

Madame Hardy, who when alive must have lived in her husband's shadow, has thus achieved immortality, at least in name. There cannot be many nicer presents for a man to give his wife.

Rose 'Madame Hardy'

BACKHOUSE NURSERY OF YORK
1816–1955

Erica carnea alba 'C. J. Backhouse'
Erica carnea alba ' James Backhouse'

Two heathers now seem to be the only commercially available cultivars commemorating a great nursery, owned and run by a famous Yorkshire family.

In 1816 James Backhouse and his brother Thomas took over an established nursery business at York. They were good businessmen, from a Quaker banking family, and over three generations the nursery flourished. Towards the end of the nineteenth century, it encompassed more than a hundred acres of prime land just to the west of York. There were blocks of greenhouses housing all sorts of tropical plants, from choice orchids to towering tree ferns, while outside were acres of fruit trees, hardy plants, and alpines.

These last were a particular speciality. On nursery land a wonderful alpine gorge in miniature was constructed, reached by a winding, wooded path. Four hundred tons of stone were used to create cliffs 25ft (7.5m) high, surrounding a placid sheet of water, and among the rocks grew thousands of alpine plants. Before ordering, prospective customers could see plants growing as if naturally, and 'The Rockwork' was also open to the public free of charge.

This amazing alpine garden was a wonderful advertisement which probably paid for itself, as teams of gardeners from the Backhouse Nursery travelled all over the country, planning, landscaping, and planting gardens for the gentry. It was they who constructed a spectacular rocky gorge for Ellen Willmott (*qv*), a most exacting customer who would accept only the best. The Backhouse Nursery became nationally known for its wonderful stock of alpines, at a time when public interest was burgeoning, and very few nurseries specialised in them.

Backhouse were also largely responsible for popularising heathers, which had been thought of as 'difficult'. One of their particular specialities was the European winter-flowering heather, *Erica carnea alba*. Richard Potter, a member of staff, was sent on a plant-hunting trip to the Italian alps, and returned with a number of selections. These were grown and stocks of the best built up.

With a flourish, in 1911, the nursery issued a magnificent suede leather-bound catalogue of heathers, complete with twenty-four beautiful colour photographs, an unheard of extravagance. 'We now have a large and unique collection which affords us pleasure to offer for the first time', they announced proudly, and assured customers that the heathers would bloom 'with cheery brightness through all the dark months of winter to the genial days of May'.

The new varieties included *Erica carnea* 'King George', still popular eighty years on, blush white *E. c.* 'C. J. Backhouse', and *E. c.* 'James Backhouse', a pale madder pink with a delicate suffusion of fawn. *Erica carnea* is one of the few heathers which does not mind chalky soil, so it is in fact particularly easy to grow. From that time, enthusiasm for heathers in private gardens has grown enormously.

Whether the nursery recouped the heavy cost of its lavish heather catalogue is unknown, but gradually the business began to decline. Great nurseries seem to need a nucleus of the family whose name they bear, and in 1921 the remaining Backhouses were bought out by a consortium of York businessmen. Things were bad during the Second World War, there was also pressure to sell the land for building, and in 1955 Backhouse of York finally closed.

A two-day sale of stock saw 4,000 young conifers, apple, pear and plum trees sold for two shillings each, and roses for £12 per hundred, buyers having to dig up their own trees and plants.

The gorge of the great 'Rockwork' had been neglected during the war years, and was finally filled in by the city's Parks Department. Now West Bank Park incorporates all that remains of the land that for nearly one and a half centuries belonged to the famous Backhouse Nursery of York.

SAM BARLOW
1825–1888

Dianthus 'Sam Barlow'
Tulipa 'Sam Barlow'

*D*ianthus 'Sam Barlow' is a much-loved garden pink, which is fitting, for it commemorates a generous, friendly man who was himself held in great affection.

Samuel Barlow was born in 1825 at Medlock Vale in Lancashire. His father's hobbies were botany and gardening, and at the age of seven young Samuel was given a shilling's worth of flower seeds and some ground on which to grow them. It was the start of a lifetime's fascination with the beauty of flowers, and by the time he was twelve he had already collected a good number of choice primroses, auriculas and pansies.

In 1847 the family moved to Castleton, near Rochdale, and Sam was employed in the bleach works where his father was manager. The hard-working, intelligent young man was eventually made a partner, and in 1861 the firm's name changed to Samuel Barlow and Co. He became a Magistrate, an Alderman of Lancashire County Council, and President of Manchester Arts Club, among other duties and honours.

The air at his home, Stakehill House, was thick with smoke from surrounding factories, but Samuel Barlow made a wonderful garden there. He had unpolluted soil brought in from Wales, and managed to grow plants of all sorts, lilies and hellebores, pansies, chrysanthemums and carnations. A contemporary declared, 'At no season of the year is Stakehill without some striking object of floral beauty, pleasing to the eye and gladdening to the heart of man'. The garden was always open, and anyone welcome to walk round.

Samuel Barlow was particularly enthusiastic about 'florists flowers', such as auriculas, polyanthus, pinks and tulips, grown by dedicated amateurs for showing in keen competition. Each year Barlow would raise as many as 500 auricula seedlings alone, selecting just two or three for further propagation, and he became known as the 'King of the Northern Florists'.

Dianthus 'Samuel Barlow' is a double white pink, with an almost chocolate-coloured centre. Although not the easiest of pinks to please, it has great character and a wonderful scent. Its nineteenth century origins are unknown—possibly it was bred at Stakehill or may simply have been named in Barlow's honour. The flower lacks the regularity that appealed to the critical eye of a florist, but Samuel Barlow was an outstanding gardener too, and he would surely have appreciated it simply as a lovely pink for the garden.

The death aged sixty-three of this cultured and big-hearted man was a sad loss to the community and to his many gardening friends. Soon afterwards a *Lobelia cardinalis* and a Korean Chrysanthemum were called after him, but they do not seem to have survived, unlike the lovely tulip that bears his name.

Tom Storer of Derby was a contemporary, famous for breeding English Florist Tulips, and when he died the seedlings in his garden were rescued by a friend, Joseph Lakin, who grew them on. One of them turned out to be a tulip of quite exceptional quality with a distinctive twisted stigma, which became 'Samuel Barlow'.

Flamed with crimson red, on a clear yellow ground, this vigorous and spectacular tulip survives thanks to enthusiasts of the English Florist Tulip. Every May when the Wakefield and North of England Tulip Society holds its Annual Show there is 'Sam Barlow' among the prize-winners, each bloom not only a thing of beauty, but an enduring symbol of the florist's skill. Samuel Barlow would surely have been pleased about that.

REV CHARLES WOLLEY DOD
1826–1904

Rose 'Wolley Dod'

O nly a few gardeners in each generation remain well known to their successors, which is inevitable but most unjust. Other talented people, quite as celebrated in their day, stay in the shadows and are gradually forgotten. At the turn of the century it was a fair bet that Gertrude Jekyll and Ellen Willmott (*qv*) would be remembered, while William Robinson (*qv*) left nothing to chance, but most keen gardeners of the time would probably have envisaged the Rev Charles Wolley Dod sharing their fame.

Charles Wolley Dod's father was the Rev J. F. Hurt, who married a Miss Wolley (pronounced 'woolly'), and adopted her name. His son Charles in due course married Frances Parker, granddaughter of Thomas Crewe Dod of Edge Hall. The Dods were an ancient Cheshire family tracing their descent back to Saxon times, and since there were no male heirs, in 1867 Charles changed his name to Wolley Dod.

After taking a degree at Cambridge, Charles taught at Eton for twenty-eight years, during which time he was ordained a Deacon by the Bishop of Lincoln. In 1878 he retired from schoolmastering, and moved to Edge Hall. He had long been interested in gardening, and now this hobby could be indulged on a large scale.

Although space was no problem, the situation was not ideal, Edge's soil being stiff clay, with poor drainage and an eager population of slugs. Over the next twenty-seven years, however, Wolley Dod created ten acres of wonderful garden, brimming with choice plants. He was a plantsman with a great zest for collecting, and an inexhaustible thirst for knowledge. It was not enough to know the name of a plant, Wolley Dod would find out its native country, its habitat, its likes and dislikes, and especially, how it could be propagated. One could not help but learn on a conducted tour of the garden, a visitor reported, just from his frequent comments. 'These do best treated as biennials; this does not come true from seed; these must be propagated by cuttings'; this is hard to transplant', etc.

Charles Wolley Dod was a man of immense intelligence and independence of mind. When you acquire a new plant, he suggested, 'without neglecting what you can learn from others about its successful cultivation, try yourself to discover something new about what soil, what aspect and surroundings suit it best. Never think you cannot cultivate a plant successfully because you cannot imitate the conditions in which it is known to thrive in its native home; you may find it flourishes still better under very different conditions which you can easily give'.

At Edge Hall every corner of the garden was utilised, even the most unpromising spots were filled with plants which appreciated just those places. Sometimes conditions matched their natural habitat, other plants were placed because Wolley Dod just had a hunch they would do well. 'Gardeners should never be content with imitating, and should not think too much about imitating nature', he declared. At Edge hardy plants could be found in island beds, and he also advocated that herbaceous borders should not automatically be dug over, ideas we tend to think of as recent.

Wolley Dod lectured at the Royal Horticultural Society, and was an acknowledged expert on daffodils. He was persuaded to contribute to the prestigious gardening magazine, 'Flora and Sylva', and his extensive knowledge, gentle humour, and huge store of practical advice still shine from his writings a hundred years later. Gertrude Jekyll held him in high regard. 'The kindest of instructors', she called him, and sent him her books in proof form, for comment and botanical corrections. The greatest gardeners of the day visited Wolley Dod at Edge Hall—people like Ellen Willmott (*qv*), Henry Harpur Crewe (*qv*), and Reginald Farrer—and he corresponded with many more.

It took a whole working day, one impressed visitor reported, to go round the garden, talking about plants with its owner. 'And,' he added, 'plants were everywhere. They line the sides of the carriage way, they fill borders upon borders, they occupy bed after bed. They clothe the slopes, they are dotted on the lawn, they edge their way in up to the very hall-door, they are invading the kitchen garden at such a rate that fruit and vegetables are ousted by their more showy looking neighbours'. 'Make a note of what you want', Wolley Dod would say enthusiastically, and plants were distributed as generously as his practical advice.

Partly as a result of this largesse, a number of plants were called after Edge Hall or its owner—there was a *Dianthus* 'Wolley Dod', a

Saxifraga 'Wolley Dod', and at least two daffodils—'Wolley Dod' and 'Edge'. All seem to have dropped out of cultivation, but although 'Wolley Dod's' Rose remains well-established, he never wrote about it, and the origin is uncertain.

'Wolley Dod's' Rose is a vigorous shrub, with semi-double, clear pink flowers and grey-green, downy leaves. The combination of the two is most attractive, and in the autumn heavy, deep red heps give a second show, again contrasting well with the foliage. It is thought to be a hybrid between *Rosa villosa* (also known as *pomifera*) and possibly an Alba garden rose, although it is often referred to simply as *Rosa villosa duplex*. Ellen Willmott included it in her great book, 'The Genus Rosa', the accompanying illustration being of an example grown at Edge Hall.

One of Charles Wolley Dod's sons, Anthony, inherited his father's interest in plants, going on plant-hunting trips, writing several erudite botanic books and pamphlets, and becoming something of an expert on roses. He never mentioned the origin of 'Wolley Dod's' Rose either, so it remains a mystery.

If the Rev Charles Wolley Dod could have been persuaded to write books about his gardening ideas and the hundreds of hardy plants he grew and knew so intimately, twentieth century gardeners would be the richer. On his death in 1904 the Gardeners' Chronicle reported sombrely, 'Truly in later times horticulture has not sustained a more severe loss than in the person of Charles Wolley Dod'. That present day gardeners have now forgotten him is our loss too.

Rev Charles Wolley Dod

REV HENRY HARPUR CREWE
1830–1883

Cheiranthus 'Harpur Crewe'
Doronicum 'Harpur Crewe'

Cheiranthus 'Harpur Crewe' is an outstanding wallflower—a two-year-old bush covered with double, sweetly scented, yolk-yellow flowers is a stunning sight. To add to the wallflower's distinction, all those now grown may well have resulted from a single source.

In the last century this wallflower flourished in the kitchen garden of Stanleys near Christchurch, the Hampshire home of Lady Crewe, widow of the ninth baronet. A yellow, double wallflower was known to exist in Elizabethan times, so the plant at Stanleys could have been a descendant, kept going through the centuries by cuttings, or it might have been a chance seedling.

Whatever the plant's origins, as it sets no seed itself, this lovely wallflower needed the attentions of someone knowledgeable to prevent it dying out. Luckily Lady Crewe had a keen gardening relation, the Reverend Henry Harpur Crewe, Rector of Drayton Beauchamp, near Tring, in Buckinghamshire. He was just the right visitor to recognise the wallflower as something special, and ensure its continuation by cuttings.

Henry Harpur Crewe's garden was said to contain one of the richest collections of hardy plants in Europe, and bulbous plants, especially crocus, were his particular enthusiasm. He must have been well-known in gardening circles, for when a green snowdrop, *Galanthus virescens*, appeared in Vienna's Botanical Garden, one of the two precious bulbs sent to England was presented to Harpur Crewe. As it multiplied he gave bulbs away, and was probably just as generous with cuttings of the special wallflower. As a result, the plant became known as 'Harpur Crewe's wallflower'. When it was put into commerce by Paul's nursery in 1896, they changed the name to *Cheiranthus* 'Harpur Crewe'.

Besides a specie crocus named in his honour, two other cultivars were called after him. There was a tall white *Aster* 'Harpur Crewe'

24

which seems to have died out, and a late-flowering *Doronicum* 'Harpur Crewe'. This bears its large, yellow daisy flowers on shorter stems than normal, making a more compact plant. It was recommended at the end of the nineteenth century as one of the best hardy plants for mixed borders. Henry Harpur Crewe must have given away so many offsets to friends that it became associated with him, but botanically it is *Doronicum plantagineum* 'Excelsum', under which name the plant is still available.

Cheiranthus 'Harpur Crewe'

MRS CATHERINE SINKINS
1837–1917

Dianthus 'Mrs Sinkins'
Dianthus 'Pink Mrs Sinkins'

Florists today are people who sell cut flowers, but this is a twentieth century meaning. For the previous two hundred years the term 'florists' referred to gardeners who concentrated on particular groups of plants. They were plant 'fanciers', who bred, developed and cosseted their treasures, exhibiting the best at highly competitive shows. Ranunculus, violas, tulips and hyacinths all went in and out of fashion as florists' flowers, but auriculas remained a steady favourite, and so did pinks.

John Thomas Sinkins was a keen florist, who at the age of forty-one became Master of Albert House, the Slough Poor Law Institution, with his wife Catherine as Matron. His workhouse duties left him time enough for his horticultural hobby, and about 1870 he developed a particularly scented white pink, with plump double flowers, and fringed petals.

Slough was also the home of the Royal Nurseries, established in the eighteenth century, and bought in 1845 by one Charles Turner. Known as the King of the Florists, Turner ran the nursery, edited a magazine called 'The Florist', and still found time to develop wonderful flowers, exhibiting them all over the country. 'He has tried no branch of floriculture without improving it', a contemporary observed admiringly. 'Had all the cups he has won been goblets, he might drink from a different chalice every day of his life'.

The nursery stocked ornamental trees, climbing and herbaceous plants, fruit trees, (he was responsible for promoting the now famous apple, Cox's Orange Pippin), and pinks in profusion. 'Charles Turner particularly directs attention to his large Stock of Carnations, Picotees, Pinks, Cloves and Perpetual-flowering Tree Carnations', his customers were told with pride.

Here was just the man to recognise outstanding qualities in a pink, and John Sinkins' new white seedling soon came to his notice. Probably flattered by the great man's attention, Sinkins agreed to sell stock of his special pink, but on one condition. It was to be named after his wife.

In 1872 *Dianthus* 'Mrs Sinkins' duly went on sale. The plant does not seem to have taken the gardening world by storm, but in 1880 Charles Turner exhibited it at the Royal Horticultural Society. There it was praised as an extremely fragrant and floriferous variety, with blooms of great size and fine form, and a First Class Certificate was awarded.

Turner died five years later, but *Dianthus* 'Mrs Sinkins' continued to increase in popularity. A really good 'doer', it makes compact, spreading clumps. The endearingly ragged white blooms are wonderfully scented, although they appear only briefly. Modern pinks now have a much extended flowering season, but 'Mrs Sinkins' has managed to retain her place as one of the best loved of all pinks. A coloured form, confusingly called 'Pink Mrs Sinkins', was developed by 1946, but never enjoyed the affection gardeners have for the original white.

Catherine Sinkins died in 1917, and her husband nine years later. In 1938, Slough became a borough, and for the town's arms a Buckinghamshire swan was chosen, holding in its beak a 'Mrs Sinkins' pink.

Mrs Catherine Sinkins

27

E. C. BUXTON
1838–1925

Anthemis tinctoria 'E. C. Buxton'
Geranium wallichianum 'Buxton's Variety'

Edmund Charles Buxton was born in Hendon, the son of a prosperous Quaker family, and great nephew of Sir Thomas Fowell Buxton, the campaigner against slavery. Little is known about Edmund's life, and why or when he moved to North Wales, but by the time his name became known in gardening circles he was living at Betwys-y-coed.

Coed Drew, his spacious home there, was set amidst magnificent scenery. A wooded mountainside rose steeply behind the house, and the large garden sloped in a series of winding paths down to the Conway, the roar of the river filling the air after heavy rain.

Buxton, a knowledgeable plantsman, contributed to gardening magazines on many topics, and had a varied and extensive circle of gardening friends, including A. T. Johnson (*qv*), who lived further down the valley. Despite high rainfall, a broad range of things thrived in the garden at Betws-y-Coed, which contained a wonderful collection of plants.

Several plants are known to have originated in E. C. Buxton's garden, including the white form of *Lamium orvala*, and a *Sedum spathulifolium* with blood crimson leaves. At least three bore his name but have not survived.

Luckily *Anthemis tinctoria* 'E. C. Buxton' has a strong will to live. *Anthemis tinctoria* is a particularly useful border plant, being hardy, and tolerant of most conditions, with yellow daisy flowers all summer. The usual colour is a strong yellow, but before the First World War Buxton had one with lemon-coloured flowers. Whether it originated as a seedling or a chance mutation is not known, but it was much admired by his many visitors, who were duly given offshoots. When a piece of this pale form reached E. A. Bowles (*qv*), he called it 'one of the delights of my garden', and the plant has retained its popularity ever since.

Primroses were easily grown at Coed Derw, enjoying the high rainfall, and in 1901 E. C. Buxton was pricking out a box of blue-flowered single primrose seedlings. Not bothering with the poorest, he was going to discard them, but his softer-hearted wife took them away to plant in the kitchen garden. Next year, going round together, they found one of these rescued plants bore double, almost turquoise blue flowers— the best double, blue primrose ever produced, according to a friend. After E. C. Buxton's death his widow sent the primrose to a great nephew, who exhibited it at the Royal Horticultural Society. *Primula vulgaris* 'Buxton's Blue' was not blessed with a strong constitution, however, and seems no longer to be with us.

Geranium wallichianum from the North Eastern Himalayas is much more robust. Introduced to this country early in the nineteenth century, its natural flower colour is a mauvey blue surrounding a white centre, but Buxton grew a much better form. This bore blooms which A. T. Johnson observed, were 'so nearly blue that it needs none of the catalogue makers licence to call them so'. It was given away generously to other gardeners, becoming known as *Geranium wallichianum* 'Buxton's Variety'. Nowadays his form has almost supplanted the original Himalayan native, and adds a valuable touch of clear blue to later summer.

In 1925, still working in his beautiful garden, E. C. Buxton was overcome by the heat of a July day and died, aged eighty-seven, mourned by numerous gardening friends. 'He was', said A. T. Johnson, 'above all else a grand old English gentleman'.

Anthemis tinctoria 'E C Buxton'

DR PHILIP MULES
1843–1905

Aubrieta 'Dr Mules'
Aubrieta 'Dr Mules Variegata'

*A*ubrieta 'Dr Mules' is probably the best known, and possibly the oldest, of all the named varieties of this popular garden plant. In a hundred years it has never been surpassed for rich colour and quality.

Philip Henry Mules studied medicine at Edinburgh, and in 1867 began practising in Dover. Four years later he moved to Bowdon on the western outskirts of Manchester, which was to be his home for the next thirty years.

As a surgeon at the Manchester Royal Eye Hospital, Mules became eminent in his field, and in 1884 was honoured by the International Congress at Paris for his work on blindness. In his spare time he gardened enthusiastically, and was fortunate in having a celebrated nursery in the locality.

William Clibran and Son of Altrincham had started in 1870 as Nurserymen, Seedsmen and Florists, and from the beginning they made a special feature of spring-flowering bulbs, bedding and herbaceous plants. 'Of this class of Plants now becoming so justly popular, we cultivate many thousands of the most showy and free flowering varieties', they informed the public proudly.

Clibrans' enthusiasm, hard work and business acumen ensured that the nursery prospered. By 1889 they had catalogues of Fruit-Trees and Roses, Shrubs, Trees, Herbaceous Plants and Bulbs, as well as an extensive seed business, and a flower shop in Central Manchester. Besides their main nursery at Altrincham, they bought a nursery in North Wales, and also established one at Bowdon, right on Dr Mules' doorstep.

At this time they could offer only two varieties of aubrieta, but, they assured customers, 'We shall be glad to purchase Seedling Plants of real merit from anyone possessing them, if they are improvements on existing varieties'.

It is thought that Philip Mules raised the outstanding aubrieta which now bears his name, and that Clibrans acquired it from him about 1894. Less rampant than many aubrietas, the flowers are of an

30

imperial purple which has never been bettered. Healthy, easy to grow, and extremely long-flowering, by 1902 the plant was hailed in the gardening press as undoubtedly the richest and deepest purple of all, and it was soon widely grown.

In 1914 Clibrans were able to announce a variegated form of *Aubrieta* 'Dr Mules', but its namesake did not live to see it. He had retired to Gresford, North Wales, in 1901, and died four years later.

Dr Philip Henry Mules

GRAVETYE AND WILLIAM ROBINSON
1838–1935

Anemone nemerosa 'Robinsoniana'
Clematis 'Gravetye Beauty'
Clematis tangutica 'Gravetye Variety'
Dianthus 'Gravetye Gem'
Geranium himalayense 'Gravetye'
Leucojum aestivum 'Gravetye Giant'
Verbena 'Gravetye'

Gravetye is a mellow, Elizabethan manor house near East Grinstead in Sussex, a country gentleman's residence which in 1885 became the prized possession of an ebullient, self-made Irishman named William Robinson.

Robinson's family in County Down were well connected but hard up, his father having run away to America with his employer's wife. So it was a very young William who began his career as a garden boy on the Marquess of Waterford's estate. Soon the tall, black-haired youngster had graduated to being a student gardener at Glasnevin, Dublin's famous Botanic Garden. Intelligent and able, he must have found his subsequent gardening job as foreman on a small country estate at Ballykilcavan frustrating and irksome. One winter's night in 1861 the twenty-three year old simply upped and left.

The story goes that, hating the tender bedding plants in his charge, Robinson doused the greenhouse boiler and opened all the windows to the frost. This is probably a highly embroidered account, for he went straight back to Glasnevin. There he sought the advice of its Director, who had no hesitation in recommending the recalcitrant young man to Robert Marnock, Curator of the Royal Botanic Society's Garden in Regent's Park, London.

Robert Marnock liked plants to look as if they were growing naturally, in contrast to the stiff, regimented fashion of the time. He was much respected, and a great influence on those who worked for him. Initially, he put Robinson in charge of a small garden devoted to native plants, but the keen youngster from Ireland swiftly rose through the ranks to become Head Gardener.

It was during his five years at Regent's Park that William Robinson discovered the power of his pen. In 1863 he made a tour of eight Botanic Gardens in the British Isles, learning about and obtaining plants. On returning he wrote a series of articles about his experiences in the influential 'Gardener's Chronicle', and soon he was a regular and notable contributor. Three years later he gave up his gardening job, learned French in seven months and took himself off to France to report for various journals on the Great Paris Exhibition of 1867.

Robinson found many things to like about French horticulture, and told his readers so, comparing British practices unfavourably. Our gardeners and nurserymen had a great deal to learn from the French, he declared forcefully, trampling on pride and sensibilities with every bulletin, and gaining notoriety in the process.

He visited the Alps and, brimming with enthusiasm for rock plants and alpine meadows, promptly wrote a book called 'Alpine Flowers for English Gardens', in which he advocated natural groupings of hardy plants 'in grove, park, copse, or by woodland walks or drives', where formality was not appropriate.

In 1870 Robinson started 'The Garden', an immensely successful magazine which ran for nearly sixty years. Many great gardeners were contributors, and it was the perfect vehicle for its editor's enthusiasms, exhortations and withering scorn. He had a burning desire to educate others, and if people disagreed with him they were not just wrong, they were fools. 'It is clear that much beauty is lost in our gardens by the stupid and ignorant practice of cutting trees into unnatural shapes', he would thunder. Topiary was not one of his enthusiasms.

He started up more magazines, and also found time to publish books, the most famous being 'The English Flower Garden', in 1883. Written 'with the co-operation of many of the Best Flower Gardeners of the Day', it was largely a description of hardy plants suitable for this country's gardens, with a plea for their placing to be more natural, and for harmony of colour and all year round interest to be considered. Of formal bedding he wrote, 'Perhaps the general reaction now going on in favour of hardy herbaceous perennial plants may quite oust the system'. In later years, and subsequent editions, he erased any mention not only of a general change of taste but of the seventy-one other contributors, thus taking all the credit himself for changing public opinion.

It was seventeen years since William Robinson had last done any

gardening himself, but his writing and some shrewd property deal-
ing had made him prosperous. In 1885, at the age of forty-seven, he
bought Gravetye Manor with 360 acres of undulating land, and set
about putting his theories into practice. Some of them were found
wanting.

Robinson had condemned terraces as artificial, but soon realised
that irregular terracing would enhance Gravetye's gentle slope.
Visitors were also taken aback to discover that the champion of
natural gardening had made formal gardens on two sides of the
house. The designs incorporated square and rectangular beds, but,
Robinson pointed out, the important thing was that the planting
was informal.

The soil was 'a nuisance', plants were flooded or died inexplicably, and a planting of 2,000 border carnations was swiftly devoured
by rabbits. William Robinson was learning that theory is no sub-
stitute for practicality.

He did however have some spectacular successes. Bulbs were
planted by the tens of thousands, and Gravetye's 'Alpine Meadow'
became a glorious sight in spring, while the idea of naturalising
daffodils and narcissus under apple trees proved completely practical. He bought extra land and planted over 500 acres of woodland,
enhancing the contours and vistas with carefully chosen species
which gave interest in summer and wonderful colour in autumn.

One of the plants which lent itself well to naturalising in the
woodland was *Anemone nemerosa* 'Robinsoniana', a large, pale
blue form of wood anemone which had originated, appropriately, in
Ireland. Mr Baxter, Curator of Oxford Botanic Garden in the
1870's, was sent some by a woman living in Ireland who wanted him
to identify it. William Robinson saw the plant growing at Oxford
soon after, and was given a piece, but exactly when his name
became officially attached to it is not clear. Other blue forms are
known, but this has the largest flowers, and William Robinson was
not alone in considering it the best and most beautiful.

In damp woodland he planted quantities of the Summer Snow-
flake, *Leucojum aestivum*. Looking like a giant snowdrop, this plant
grows wild in Europe, and around Limerick a particularly fine,
large-flowered form was known to exist. William Robinson may
have been given bulbs on one of his visits to Ireland, for his
leucojum also had bigger flowers than usual, and several to a stem.
He gave plants away to visitors and friends and it became known as
Leucojum aestivum 'Gravetye Giant'.

Formal areas were planted with such things as violas, carnations and geraniums. The geranium which takes its name from the garden is a shorter-growing form of *G. himalayense* (formerly *G. grandiflorum*). *Geranium himalayense* 'Gravetye' is a sun-loving border plant with large purple flowers in early summer, but its origin is unknown. It could well have been brought by one of the many visitors to Gravetye, for William Robinson knew everyone in the gardening world.

He still retained links with many French nurserymen, and one of them, F. Morel of Lyons, was fascinated by clematis, an enthusiasm that Robinson came to share. Using *Clematis texensis* as one parent, Morel conducted some experimental breeding, and just before the First World War sent a number of the resultant seedlings to Gravetye.

Robinson employed more than a dozen gardeners, and in 1910 twenty-nine year old Ernest Markham joined the staff, later rising to be Head Gardener. He became an expert on clematis, and was particularly impressed by one of Morel's hybrids. A strong-growing plant bearing numerous red, tulip-shaped flowers, this was exhibited in 1935 as *Clematis* 'Gravetye Beauty', and with its vigour and hardiness has proved perennially popular. *Clematis tangutica* 'Gravetye Variety' is much less distinctive, only having fresher green foliage, and lighter-coloured flowers than the type.

The enlarged estate encompassed several farms, and in 1925 Robinson offered land to Walter Ingwersen, a distinguished alpine specialist then working with Clarence Elliott at Six Hills Nursery (*qv*). Ingwersen's Birch Farm Nursery soon became one of the best known alpine nurseries in the country, stocking a great range of plants. This included small pinks, and one seedling with a low-growing habit and single, maroon and white flowers, was named *Dianthus* 'Gravetye Gem'.

When he was seventy, William Robinson had a fall which left him partially paralysed, and he was also found to be suffering from syphilis. Confined to a wheelchair for the rest of his life, he acquired a large Citroen vehicle with caterpillar tracks. In this he could still tour the estate and keep an eye on the garden, now in the full charge of Ernest Markham and his staff. Robinson received numerous visitors, and was offered a knighthood by Ramsay MacDonald in 1933, which with creditable, and unusual, modesty he turned down. 'I feel I must leave life as I entered it', he replied.

The abrasive William Robinson was by then almost revered as the man who single-handedly turned British gardening away from Victorian stiffness—the 'Father of the English Flower Garden'. It was a view he greatly encouraged, and since he outlived most of his contemporaries there was no-one to dispute it. More recently it has been said of him that he never jumped on a bandwagon until it had been rolling for at least ten years. As he was a born publicist, however, any bandwagon with William Robinson aboard was bound to gather speed.

On his death in 1935, aged ninety-seven, Gravetye was left to the nation. The woods were to be used for forestry, under strict conditions, and the house and garden opened to the public one day a week. Inevitably, over the years the gardens became neglected, and it is only since the house became a hotel and country club, in 1968, that restoration of the garden has been undertaken.

William Robinson

REV WILLIAM WILKS
1843–1923

Papaver rhoeas 'Shirley Poppies'

The Reverend William Wilks was an illustrious member of that well known Victorian breed, gardening churchmen. He came from a family of keen gardeners, and his Kent childhood was strongly tinged with memories of his father's and grandfather's talk of plants, and gardening friends. Young William's own interest in the natural world can only have been increased by having two of Charles Darwin's sons as schoolfriends, but after an MA at Cambridge, he went into the Church.

At the age of thirty-six Wilks became Vicar of Shirley, near Croydon, now overtaken by London spread, but in 1879 a country village. A keen and active member of the Royal Horticultural Society by then, William Wilks began at once to improve the vicarage garden. His ideas indicate that here was a gardener of talent. He strived for a garden 'with abundant variety of form and colour, of flower and foliage; a garden in which every day finds something fresh to look at, to admire, to watch; a garden where every step brings variety and every season its own especial charm; a garden not only to take pleasure in, but to be itself a pleasure'.

This could not of course be accomplished all at once, and a year after moving in, part of the garden abutting the fields was still full of weeds and wild flowers, including the red field poppy, *Papaver rhoeas*. The observant Wilks noticed that one poppy, instead of being completely scarlet, had a narrow edging of white to the petals. He marked that bloom, saved the seed and sowed it.

Next year, out of the resulting two hundred plants, he had four or five on which all the flowers had white edging. The best of these were selected, the seed saved, and so on, for several years. Each summer the poppies showed a larger infusion of white or pink, until he arrived at quite a pale pink, and one absolutely pure white.

This would have been sensational enough for most men, but William Wilks then set himself a further goal. He was determined to eliminate the dark centre of the flower—to change the base of each petal, the stamens, anthers and stigmas from black to yellow or white.

His patient persistence had its reward. 'I have succeeded at last in obtaining a strain with petals varying from the brightest scarlet to pure white', he was able to report in 1900, 'with all shades of pink in between, and with all possible variations of flakes and edged flowers.' From the flower centre to the tip of each petal, the transformation of the field poppy was complete.

By this time he had been Secretary of the Royal Horticultural Society for twelve years. When he was elected in 1888, it was in dire straits. No longer the leading exponent of horticultural excellence, education and improvement, its Chiswick garden had become a mere pleasure ground, with expensive statuary, tennis courts, and a skating rink available to the public. The Society had lost its way, membership fell and the financial position became alarming. In 1885 a new Treasurer, Sir Trevor Lawrence was appointed, determined to turn the ship round, and he was soon joined by the Reverend William Wilks, who served as Secretary for the next thirty-two years.

Together they reformed and rebuilt the Society, moved it to cheaper premises, restarted the Journal, organised lectures and fortnightly shows, and instituted a two-day Great Spring Show, early forerunner of the Chelsea Flower Show.

William Wilks was the ideal man for the job of Secretary. A strong personality, he was blessed with humour, diplomacy and powers of persuasion, as well as the determination and vision that he applied to breeding his poppies. It was said of him that he aspired and inspired, but he also worked. The result was that by the turn of the century the Society's membership had quadrupled and its financial position was sound. The Royal Horticultural Society had regained its position as leading authority in the horticultural world, and as such, in 1903, was given by the generous Sir Thomas Hanbury, sixty acres of land at Wisley for a garden.

William Wilks was not a wealthy man, but he refused to make any money from his astonishing Shirley poppies. When blooms were shown at a Royal Horticultural Society Show in 1901, they were unanimously voted a First Class Certificate, but their raiser made no attempt to sell the seed. 'I am proud of my poppies', he said, 'because i) they are known all over the world, ii) the seed has been given away freely to whomsoever has asked, and iii) they have given joy and delight to the poorest as well as the richest'.

His quest for the perfect poppy had required not only determination and dedication, but also the ruthlessness to eliminate any blooms that were inferior. 'To prevent these infecting the better ones', he reported, 'I am about among my flowers between three and four o'clock in the morning, so as to pull up, and trample on, and destroy, the bad ones before the bees have a chance of conveying pollen to others.'

It is probably just as well that the Rev William Wilks was a much-loved and respected churchman, with no question mark as to his mental stability. One can imagine a neighbour, wakened in the small hours of a summer morning, getting up and drawing his curtains to establish the source of the disturbance. After gazing a moment he could return to bed, reporting laconically to his wife, 'Vicar's out there, trampling on the flowers again'.

Papaver rhoeas 'Shirley Poppies'

CANON JAMES WENT
1845–1936

Linaria purpurea 'Canon Went'

Linaria purpurea 'Canon Went' is a pink form of the tall, spikey, purple linaria which grows wild in Southern Europe. *L.p.* 'Canon Went' does not seed quite as prolifically as the common variety, and its elegant spires of soft pink, coupled with the unusual name, make it a plant held in much affection.

James Went was born in 1845 in Worcester, where his father was a tailor, and attended the King's School. There he first suffered under the regime of an abysmal headmaster, and then experienced the school's complete metamorphosis when he was replaced by one of the best in the school's history. The contrasting effects of good and bad headmasters were not lost on the young James Went, who decided to go into the teaching profession himself.

His first job after leaving school at eighteen was as master in a preparatory school in Great Malvern. Whilst teaching there he obtained a 'steamboat' degree at Trinity College, Dublin—this entailed studying at home, and taking the packet steamer to Dublin each year, to register at Trinity College and to take examinations.

He was ordained in 1868 and then taught classics at Nottingham High School, followed by a senior appointment at Bradford Grammar School for six years.

In 1877 Wyggeston Hospital Boys' School opened in Leicester, and the thirty-two year old James Went was appointed Headmaster. For the next forty-three years, under his intelligent and humane rule, the school prospered and was soon renowned for academic excellence. Went was highly regarded in the profession, wrote a book about his experiences as Headmaster, and became Vice President of the Association of Headmasters.

A short, energetic man with hooded, piercing eyes and bushy side-whiskers, he can only have been called 'Jimmy' behind his back, but when, in 1919, he was succeeded by a man named Thomas Kingdom, irrepressible school graffiti read, 'Jimmy Went, Kingdom Come'

On his retirement James Went was made an Honorary Canon of Leicester Cathedral and a Freeman of the City. In 1936 he died, aged 89, and at his memorial service an Air Marshal flew over the school and dipped in salute to his old headmaster.

No plants of *Linaria purpurea* 'Canon Went' now grow in the garden of his old cottage at Birstall, Leicester, and he did not include gardening among his stated hobbies. James Went did however enjoy travelling. Possibly he found the pink-flowered form in Europe and brought seed home, but usually only keen gardeners indulge in such eccentric behaviour. It seems more likely that a gardening friend raised or found the plant, and named it in honour of a much-respected headmaster.

Canon James Went

TRESEDERS AND BISHOP HUGHES OF LLANDAFF
1847–1938

Dahlia 'Bishop of Llandaff'

S ome garden plants are loved for their outstanding qualities, others partly because they have intriguing names. *Dahlia* 'Bishop of Llandaff' qualifies for popularity on both these counts.

Llandaff, an ancient cathedral city situated on the River Taff in Wales, has now become a part of Cardiff. And it was to Cardiff that nurseryman Stephen Treseder of Truro moved his family in the 1840's. He leased a large acreage from the Marquis of Bute, and in 1850 his son William started a nursery of his own on some of the land. William prospered, expanding the business, and in due course his sons in turn became involved in the nursery.

One of them, Fred Treseder, was particularly interested in dahlias, and for fifty years experimented with their cultivation and breeding. About 1924 he presented blooms from four or five of his best seedlings that year to his good friend the Rt Rev Joshua Pritchard Hughes, Bishop of Llandaff.

The bishop's own enthusiasm tended towards the temperance movement, and strict observance of the Sabbath (on which day he refused to use any form of transport). Gardening does not seem to have featured in his life, but he selected as the best dahlia a striking bloom, which Fred Treseder decided to name after him.

Bishop Hughes had chosen a dahlia which turned out to be rather special. The simple, semi-double flowers are a rich and satisfying scarlet, with a dark centre, and whereas most dahlias have bright green leaves, the Bishop has dark purple foliage.

This beautiful plant came about by pure luck, according to Fred Treseder. 'We are always experimenting', he said. 'In this case we do not know the parents—it originated from a batch of "chance" seedlings'. He tried sowing seeds of his outstanding dahlia, but they did not produce anything spectacular. 'In one year we had 5,000 seedlings from this plant', he reported, 'but none has excelled the parent.'

Treseders exhibited *Dahlia* 'Bishop of Llandaff' at the Royal

Horticultural Society in 1928. It received an Award of Merit, and the plant caught the imagination of the gardening world. Twelve years later it was more extensively grown than any other variety, and plants of it had been sent to countries as diverse as Germany, America, Czechoslovakia, Australia and New Zealand. 'The most popular flower of the moment in many parts of England in any test is the dahlia known as the "Bishop of Llandaff"', recorded The Spectator in 1936.

Besides having a most attractive flower and purple foliage, 'The Bishop of Llandaff' was to prove special in another respect. It seemed to be immune to a virus which commonly attacks dahlias. Dahlia specialists began to suspect, however, that although showing no symptoms itself, the Bishop harboured the virus and passed it on to others. This made the plant something of a pariah, and after a while dahlia fanciers ceased to grow it.

From being a fashionable phenomenon, 'Bishop of Llandaff' slipped into obscurity as the years went by. The plant became very hard to find, until in the 1980's Treseder's distinctive dahlia began to enjoy a resurgence of popularity, as gardeners wanting to make a 'red' border sought it out.

Star quality makes this a plant often grown by people who profess not to like dahlias, just as it was in the 1930's. 'Personally, I do not care for dahlias in general', wrote a distinguished journalist in 1936, 'some of them are positively alarming, so big are they and heavy and brilliant. The Bishop is as bright as a flame, but it is not alarming, and the dark purplish foliage topped by the scarlet flowers is a triumph of combination.'

Bishop Hughes, the non-gardener who knew a good dahlia when he saw one, retired to Sussex in 1931, and died seven years later. William Treseder Ltd is still in business, now selling cut flowers in a chain of shops, and proud to have a garden centre and head office on the very spot where William Treseder started his Cardiff nursery in 1850.

THE SHASTA DAISY AND LUTHER BURBANK
1849–1926

The Shasta Daisy

Shasta County in Northern California takes its name from the region's Mount Shasta, but Shasta Daisies are not wild flowers of that area, nor anywhere else for that matter. They were the deliberate creation of Luther Burbank, entrepreneur, genius and plant breeder extraordinary.

When young, Luther Burbank was deeply impressed by Charles Darwin's book, 'The Variation of Animals and Plants Under Domestication'. It convinced him that fruit, flowers and vegetables could be improved dramatically by intelligent selection and breeding.

His New England home was an important potato-growing area, and while still in his twenties Luther Burbank was able to produce the Burbank potato, a great improvement on the local variety. Sales of it gave him enough money to move to Santa Rosa in California where he set up a plant breeding station, raising over a million plants a year.

Scientists tended to scoff at this untrained, freethinking and confident man, especially at his unusual advertisements. In 1884 he offered in his local newspaper '500,000 vigorous Fruit and Nut Trees growing in our two nurseries at Santa Rosa . . . DON'T BE FOOLED . . . Come and See. Catalogs will soon be ready. Luther Burbank.'

'Given time, patience and a knowledge of Nature's Law man can modify, change, improve, add or take away from, any plant he chooses', Burbank declared, and over the years he proceeded to do just that, confounding the sceptics. Improved varieties of apples, melons, lilies, peas and sweetcorn, even a stoneless plum, were among the hundreds he marketed. Often he would literally 'create' a vegetable or fruit to order. His catalogues, called 'New Creations in Fruit and Flowers', offered the improved varieties for sale together with complete rights and exclusive control.

Burbank was not popular with some religious leaders, but his achievements and homely philosophy laced with salty humour won him friends worldwide. His birthday was set aside as a Californian State Holiday, a portrait of Burbank appeared on America's widely-used three cent stamp in 1904, and he became known as The Wizard of Horticulture. But Luther Burbank was a scientist, not a magician. 'You cannot make the peony bear wheat nor the ivy produce roses', he explained. 'What you can do is give the peony sturdiness, variegated colour, the power to grow taller, or the habit of growing dwarfed; you can give the ivy some few new habits, within a limited range, but surely and definitely'.

When Burbank moved to California in 1875 he took with him the wild New England ox-eye daisy to plant in his garden, as a reminder of home. After a while he decided to try increasing the size of flower, and crossed it with the European ox-eye daisy. Some of the resulting hybrids were an improvement, but not wholly satisfactory. At this point he heard of a Japanese daisy with small but brilliantly white, waxy flowers, ordered some, and stirred them into his melting pot of genes.

For the next six years he grew thousands of seedlings, each year selecting only the best, and around 1890 had produced a plant 'graceful enough to please the eye and hardy enough to live in any soil; with flowers 3–6in (7–15cm) in diameter, of crystal whiteness and borne on long graceful stems'. It was, he announced, 'a daisy that surpassed my dreams: the Shasta'.

Luther Burbank died in 1926 and is buried under a cedar of Lebanon in his garden, now publicly owned. Later plant breeders went on to produce fringed and double forms of his flower, so that nurseries no longer stock his original, single, Shasta daisy. It remains a memorial to him, however, in countless gardens—hardy, healthy, long-flowering and eager to cover new ground.

MADAME CAROLINE TESTOUT

Rose 'Climbing Madame Caroline Testout'

Madame Caroline Testout was a late nineteenth century French couturiere from Grenoble, the proprietor of fashionable salons in London and Paris. She regularly visited Lyons, where she purchased silks, and that city happened also to be an important centre for rose-growing. Hybrid Tea roses were at that time all the rage, breeders having at last been able to develop them successfully, and no rose nurseryman was more celebrated than 'The Wizard of Lyons', Joseph Pernet-Ducher.

Mme Testout was obviously an astute businesswoman who understood the value of good publicity, and she went to see Pernet-Ducher, asking if one of his new roses could be named after her. He agreed, although not with her choice of seedling which he considered mediocre. The nursery's reputation might suffer from producing a poor rose by the hundreds, but his customer stood firm and a deal was struck. The rose duly made its debut at the salon's 1890 Spring Fashion Show, bearing the name 'Madame Caroline Testout'.

Although not strong on scent, it was an immediate success with Madame Testout's well-to-do customers, and with the gardening public, for its abundant silky, rose-pink flowers. Only two years after the rose's introduction the Royal Horticultural Society gave it an Award of Merit. Four years later the Reverend H. J. Pemberton, Vice President of the National Rose Society no less, and a successful rose breeder himself, declared, 'In my opinion it is one of the best, if not the very best, new rose of the last seven years'.

The new variety's popularity spread to America, and it has been estimated that in the town of Portland in Oregon, nearly half a million bushes of 'Caroline Testout' were planted along the sidewalks. Not surprisingly, it was dubbed The Rose City.

In 1901 a climbing form of this rose appeared, and eventually became more popular than the bush rose, which is no longer commercially available.

Whether or not Caroline Testout's dressmaking business actually

46

flourished as a result of her namesake's success is not recorded. And perhaps Madame Pernet-Ducher observed the rose's popularity with mixed feelings. At any rate, only a year after giving 'Caroline Testout' to the world, her husband named one of his new roses 'Madame Pernet-Ducher'. The semi-double flower of this rose was cream, edged with lemon, which sounds attractive. But alas, it caused not a ripple of interest and in a few years sank without trace, as did so many other new varieties. Life can be hard on the wives of rose breeders.

Rose 'Madame Caroline Testout'

MRS R. O. BACKHOUSE
1857–1921

Galanthus 'Backhouse Spectacles'
Galanthus 'Mrs Backhouse'
Lilium 'Mrs R. O. Backhouse'
Narcissus 'Mrs R. O. Backhouse'

Robert Ormston Backhouse came from a daffodil-fancying family. William, his father, was a Durham banker distantly related to the Backhouses of York (*qv*), and one of the first people in this country to breed narcissus systematically. After William's death in 1869 most of his seedlings were bought by the bulb specialist Peter Barr, but when Robert married seventeen years later he still had some of his father's collection. He and his wife went to live at Sutton Court, near Hereford, and a walled garden was built in which to plant the remaining narcissus.

It was not long before these originals were joined by the results of the couple's own crossings, for Sarah Elizabeth Backhouse was also a keen and clever hybridist. Their ambition was to produce a long-trumpeted narcissus (daffodil) with a red or dark orange trumpet. As a result of this quest they bred many brightly coloured short-cupped narcissi which became popular, and won numerous show prizes.

In 1905 Mrs Backhouse exhibited, to gasps of admiration, a narcissus with a white perianth and a long cup of shell-pink. It proved to be very slow to reproduce, and was only introduced to commerce by Peter Barr eighteen years later, at the astronomical price of £40 per bulb. The unusual flower was named *Narcissus* 'Mrs R. O. Backhouse', after its raiser who had died two years earlier in 1921.

Mrs Backhouse was particularly interested in bulbous plants, and tried her hand at breeding colchicums, crocus, hyacinths and hardy agapanthus, but probably her greatest success was with lilies. A Dutch breeder had experimented by crossing a white Martagon lily with *Lilium hansonii*. Mrs Backhouse made the same cross but reversed the parents, and achieved a range of lilies with very good qualities indeed.

Vigorous and healthy, the Backhouse Hybrids are stem-rooting, so that they can be planted deeply; fairly lime-tolerant; and extremely long-lived. They produce spires of flowers shaped like Turk's caps in colours ranging from cream and yellow to orange and purple-red, with a peppering of dark spots inside each bloom. One, a pale yellow with pink shading and purple spots, was named after Sutton Court, and a pale orange became *Lilium* 'Mrs R. O. Backhouse'. Another commemorates her son, William Ormston Backhouse, who carried on his parents' hybridising work with both lilies and daffodils. Unfortunately Backhouse lilies are slow to reproduce, making them expensive, and nowadays they are also difficult to come by.

A large collection of snowdrops was built up at Sutton Court, and the Backhouses tried crossing good forms of the common *Galanthus nivalis* with the Crimean snowdrop, *G. plicatus*. The progeny had attractively large flowers but were unfortunately only short-lived. The origins are unknown of the snowdrop that became known as *Galanthus* 'Mrs Backhouse' but it is tall and sturdy, with rather rounded petals, like *G.* 'Sam Arnott'.

Another snowdrop from Sutton Court, the quaintly named *Galanthus* 'Backhouse Spectacles' is not easily distinguishable from *G.* × *atkinsii*, but it is quite tall-growing, with a typical triangular shape to the flowers. The story goes that Mrs Backhouse had been admiring a particular clump of snowdrops, and afterwards when she went into the house, missed her glasses. They were found where she had left them, beside the snowdrop clump, which then became known as the 'spectacles' snowdrop. Later, when bulbs of it were given away, the name went with them.

Mrs Backhouse died in 1921, but her husband continued to live at Sutton Court for another nineteen years, still hybridising enthusiastically, and above all carrying on the quest for a red-trumpeted daffodil. Aged 86, he died in his bath chair one day whilst going round his beloved garden—a gardener's perfect exit.

GEORGE RUSSELL
1857–1951

Russell Lupins

In 1937 the Royal Horticultural Society awarded one of its highest honours, the Veitch Memorial Medal, to a jobbing gardener from Yorkshire named George Russell. It was official recognition of his achievement in producing a strain of lupins that had created a sensation in the gardening world. Although medals make news at the time, they are soon forgotten. The lupins themselves made a far better memorial to this modest, patient man who devoted years of his life to one flower.

George Russell was born at Stillington, a small village a few miles from York, where his father was a cobbler, and one of his early memories was of being taken to a local flower show, and seeing vases of blue and white lupins. They would almost certainly have been *Lupinus polyphyllus*, a native of North America, introduced to Britain in 1826. The flowers are varying shades of blue, with the occasional white, and the sight of them seems to have made an impression on the young George Russell.

Not much is certain about his early life, as he preferred not to talk about it. He is known, however, to have worked for various nurseries, including Pennells of Lincoln, and Backhouse of York (*qv*), specialising in plants grown under glass. He married, and just one child survived, a son who was not close to his father. The family lived in Kensington Street, York, and when his wife became ill, George Russell turned to jobbing gardening in and around York. The more flexible hours enabled him to nurse her, which he did devotedly until she died. Amongst his employers was a certain Mrs Micklethwaite, and in 1911, when George Russell was 54, his attention was caught by a vase of lupins she had arranged. Evidently he did not think much of it, and decided that the flower could do with improving.

Russell already grew fruit and vegetables on two allotments, and dabbled in hybridising flowers such as daffodils and aquilegias. Now he began filling two more allotments with lupins, making a start by buying plants or seed of every known variety. Russell probably had little formal education, but he was a highly intelligent man, with a great thirst for knowledge. He rose at five every morning and read two newspapers before leaving for work, and he knew all about Mendel's experiments in plant breeding.

Patiently George Russell selected only the best lupin flowers each year, breeding from them and discarding the rest. If he happened on any tree lupins growing in the surrounding area, he quietly destroyed those too, to prevent their pollen from affecting his plants. Only bumble-bees are heavy enough to pull open the lupin's 'keel' and work the flower, and Russell left much of the pollination to them. He also hybridised by hand, covering the spikes afterwards with the muslin liners from hundredweight sugar bags.

Besides producing new colours, George Russell sought to alter the shape of the common lupin. He wanted the individual flowers to be larger and closer together, with the bell-shaped 'keels' fat enough to hide the central stalk, thus creating a solid looking spike.

After his wife's death, Russell was looked after by a kindly next door neighbour, Mrs Heard, whose young boy, Sonny, was suffering from TB. Plenty of fresh air was prescribed, so George Russell took the youngster with him on all his gardening jobs, and also up to the allotments, where in the summer they worked among the lupins till dark.

For twenty-three years he persevered in developing the flowers, crossing and recrossing, and word spread of this unusual allotment, ablaze with lupins as they had never been seen before. The possibilities of improving the lupin had occupied other nurserymen, and several had developed different colours. Only George Russell, however, achieved not only a wonderful range of colours but a solid spike where the central stalk was completely obscured by flowers.

Nurserymen and representatives of seed companies from all over the country, even from abroad, came to York and offered large sums for seeds or plants. They met with a polite but unwavering refusal. Russell had not yet achieved the perfection he had set himself, and in any case was not doing it for money. As time went on and he approached his eighties, increasing numbers of nurserymen appealed to him to sell, lest the secret of his wonderful lupins be lost to posterity. Russell had an answer to that. Sonny Heard, he said, knew all there was to know, and the offers were steadfastly refused.

In 1934 a nurseryman named Jimmy Baker, something of a character himself, went to see the old man to try and persuade him that the world ought to have these wonderful flowers. Bakers Nursery already offered quite a good selection of lupins, and he was probably looked on with more favour as a result. 'I don't want to sell my lupins', Russell told him, 'but I have got a figure in my head'. If you can hit that exactly, they're yours'. Baker made his offer, and it was indeed spot on. A deal was agreed whereby the lupins changed hands; Sonny should be given a job for life; and Russell's quest for perfection was to continue.

By 1936 5,000 of Russell's lupin seedlings were growing at Boningale, part of Bakers Nursery, near Wolverhampton. A cottage nearby had been offered, but initially Russell preferred to remain at York. It had been agreed however that he should 'rogue' the seedlings, selecting for growing on only those that met his exacting standards. A car was duly sent to York to fetch the old man, and Jimmy Baker must have been aghast when Russell destroyed no fewer than 4,200 of his 5,000 valuable seedlings that first year.

At last, in 1937 Bakers Nursery was ready to exhibit Russell Lupins for the first time. They caused a sensation. The display won a Gold Medal, and led to the Royal Horticultural Society honouring the eighty-year old George Russell. A year later Bakers announced, 'Seeds of the World Famous Russell Lupin are now available for your garden, the result of twenty years patient endeavour and devotion'. Just twelve seeds cost a shilling, and every packet of Russell Lupin seed was sealed with a picture of George Russell. 'This is your guarantee', the nursery assured customers, 'refuse any packets which are not so sealed'.

Russell never took cuttings to perpetuate particular plants, his quest had been for better strains every year from seed. Now Bakers began to propagate vegetatively the best of their stock, selling them under such names as 'Sonny' (cerise); 'Mrs Micklethwaite' (salmon pink); and 'City of York' (a bright red). Many Russell Lupins are bi-coloured, the 'keel' and 'standard' part of each flower being of contrasting colours. It was one of these, a pink with creamy white, which George Russell chose to bear his own name.

For many years the old man continued to work with Jimmy Baker, creating still better lupins. After the war, when Sonny Heard left the forces, married and settled with his wife into a cottage at Bakers Nursery, George Russell came to live with them. He was awarded an MBE in 1951 for his services to horticulture, and died just a few months afterwards, aged 94. He was buried in Boningale's tiny churchyard, in an unmarked grave with no fuss, as he would have wished. He hated wreaths. 'I'll give you all the flowers you want when you're alive', he used to tell people, 'but not a single one when you're dead'.

Lupins are not long-lived, and today very few of the original named varieties survive in a healthy state, many being either wrongly named, or virus-ridden. The plant also produces seed copiously, and most so-called Russell Lupins now are simply inferior seedlings.

Today Mrs Pat Edwards, owner of what was Baker's Nursery, holds the National Collection of Russell Lupins, and is working to improve the strain again. Advised by Sonny Heard, now in his seventies, she is using exactly the same methods as George Russell, over seventy years ago.

George Russell

WARLEY PLACE AND
ELLEN WILLMOTT
1858–1934

Aethionema 'Warley Rose'
Campanula cochlearifolia 'Miss Willmott'
Eryngium giganteum 'Miss Willmott's Ghost'
Rose 'Ellen Willmott'
Scabiosa caucasia 'Miss Willmott'
Veronica prostrata 'Miss Willmott'

M iss Ellen Willmott, one of the great characters of British gardening, was the clever and headstrong daughter of a well-to-do London solicitor. In 1875 he moved with his wife and two daughters from London to Warley Place, near Brentwood in Essex. The house stood high on hilly ground, and the small estate was blessed with stately trees, a stream and several natural ponds. In time, neighbouring land was also added. The Willmott family were all keen on gardening, but it was the elder daughter Ellen who was most interested, throwing her prodigious energy into making the new garden.

Dedicated to plants and gardening, and becoming formidably knowledgeable, Ellen was soon mixing with the elite of the horticultural world. Visits were exchanged with the gardening luminaries of her day. Never one to trouble much about the sensibilities of others, she is said to have surreptitiously scattered the seed of plants she thought were unjustifiably missing from those gardens she visited. A favourite for this purpose was the slow-germinating, silvery sea holly, *Eryngium giganteum*, with the charming result that it became known as 'Miss Willmott's Ghost'.

She was a strong and complex character, but not by all accounts terribly likeable. The Willmott family wealth had been made in trade, and maybe this fuelled her aggressive striving for recognition in both horticultural and social spheres.

Ellen Willmott became an expert on roses, producing a lengthy and authoritative book, The Genus Rosa—dedicated to Queen Alexandra—which set out to provide a systematic botanical record of rose species. She wrote the general description of each rose and an account of its source and history, while commissioning the distinguished botanical artist Alfred Parsons to produce illustrations. It was a task which took years and a great deal of money to complete. The plant explorer E. H. Wilson named *Rosa willmottiae* after her in 1904, but, in view of her interest and expert knowledge, it is surprising that more hybrids were not named in her honour. As it was, the cream-coloured hybrid tea rose 'Ellen Willmott' was only launched in 1936, two years after her death.

Miss Willmott supported various plant expeditions financially, receiving seeds and plant material in return, thus many species new to this country became associated with her and Warley.

Vast sums were also spent at nurseries—one nurseryman revealed that from 1890 to 1900 she used to spend some £1,500 a year buying plants from him, and he was not alone in appreciating her custom. No wonder nurserymen honoured so important a buyer by dedicating a whole host of new varieties to her.

Some namesakes, for example white *Scabiosa caucasia* 'Miss Willmott', proved to be outstanding plants that are still grown today, while others such as *Iris* 'Miss Willmott', *Aster* 'Miss Willmott' and *Verbena grandiflora* 'Ellen Willmott' are no longer stocked by nurseries. Of over fifty different cultivars named after her or Warley, less than a dozen are thought to exist today. The idea of complimenting a good customer could backfire too. A mauve-blue phlox named 'Ellen Willmott' was humiliatingly dismissed as 'badly subject to mildew' after trials at Wisley; and contemporary gardener E. A. Bowles (*qv*), referring to a carnation that bore her name, once wrote mischievously, '"Ellen Willmott" requires disbudding and fussing over beyond our practice'.

New plants were also developed in her own garden, and Miss Willmott would put them up to the Royal Horticultural Society in the hope of an Award. *Veronica prostrata* 'Warley Blue' was voted down in 1914, but nearly eighty years later it is still sold commercially, although the name has mutated to *V.p.* 'Miss Willmott'. The veronica's survival vindicates her judgement over that of the Royal Horticultural Society judges, which would have pleased but not surprised her.

She sat on several RHS Committees herself, but tended to be dismissive of her colleagues' knowledge. Every member of each of the committees should pass an examination on their special subject, she maintained, before being allowed to sit in judgement on the plants brought forward. It was her practice to wear as a buttonhole some unusual flower, and she took a subtle delight in discovering how many committee men failed to identify it. To those as knowledgeable as herself, however, she could be a charming and generous friend.

Weeding at Warley Place had to be done Miss Willmott's way, and she used to inspect the trugs of the less experienced gardeners, picking out anything that was not a weed in her understanding. Self-sown seedlings, provided they were not going to harm their neighbours, were not weeds, and this policy resulted in a number of the 'Warley' varieties. When a seedling aethionema appeared in the garden, with greater vigour and earlier rose pink flowers than any other, Miss Willmott's eagle eye was quick to spot that it was rather special. This time the judging committee of the RHS unanimously agreed, and *Aethionema* 'Warley Rose' has become one of the most famous of Miss Willmott's plants.

Although both rich and attractive, she was too forceful to have married easily. Instead, after inheriting Warley Place entirely in 1898, she poured money into creating a garden to gasp at. The Alpine Garden, constructed as a rocky gorge by the Backhouse Nursery of York (*qv*), became famous. It occupied over an acre, and at the bottom flowed a stream running down to a lake. 'It is not a garden', exclaimed one alpine enthusiast, 'it is a valley hollowed in the mountains, and in this valley is shown a synthesis of the whole flora of mountainous regions. Hidden among the masses of flowers, one feels as if transported into the midst of the great landscapes of Scotland or the Alps of Switzerland'.

In spring the lawns of Warley Place were carpeted with a myriad bulbs—Miss Willmott grew 600 species and varieties of narcissus alone. A walled garden was given over to plants that needed extra shelter, there were trial grounds, artistically-planted borders, shady Rose Walks and a Water Garden. 'Every foot of ground is occupied by some plant which desires that spot and no other for its full contentment', an impressed visitor reported in 1900.

Any new introduction that appealed to her for its beauty and interest was acquired, multiplied and grown to perfection. If it failed to please, however, it was ruthlessly evicted, for she planted according to her own taste and inclination.

At its peak, Warley Place is said to have required the attentions of 104 uniformed gardeners. It was a magnificent garden which won world renown—even royalty came to visit. As if possession of such a place was not enough, Miss Willmott also bought a grand house in

Italy and another in France, around which to make spectacular gardens.

The scale of her extravagance on all sides is hard to grasp. She was enormously wealthy, but it is not surprising that under the onslaught of such reckless spending her fortune melted away. Land had to be sold off and staff dismissed. Towards the end of her life the garden at Warley Place, though severely reduced, was still beautiful, and still stocked with thousands of rare plants. But it was not gardening on the royal scale of past years, and Ellen Willmott died a resentful and saddened old woman in 1934.

The garden was soon plundered and neglected, as the house stood empty and was then demolished in favour of several planned smaller houses. In fact, as a result of Green Belt policy, these were never built, and gradually the garden reverted to woodland.

In 1977, more than forty years after her death, the land was leased to the Essex Naturalists' Trust which now runs it as a nature reserve. Left to themselves, daffodils, snowdrops and scillas have multiplied gloriously under the trees, but there is now little to indicate the splendour of the garden at Warley Place created by Miss Ellen Willmott.

Miss Ellen Willmott

BLANCHE HEGARTY
1860–1929

Schizostylis coccinea 'Mrs Hegarty'

'Coccinea' means 'scarlet', and *Schizostylis coccinea*, the Kaffir Lily from South Africa, lives up to its Latin epithet, bearing bright red, gladiolus-like flowers in early autumn. So when, in 1921, a pink form, named *Schizostylis coccinea* 'Mrs Blanche Hegarty', was exhibited at the Royal Horticultural Society's Show in London, it caused quite a stir.

Blanche Hegarty was a doctor's wife at Clonbur in Ireland's County Galway, where she had been born and brought up. A keen gardener, she lived with her husband and four children in a Georgian house named 'Poleska'. The garden was not large, but in it surfaced an underground stream which enabled her to make water features, and she grew a great variety of plants. It must have been a lovely garden, even inspiring a poem about it by Katherine Tynan.

As plantsmen do, Blanche swapped plants with other gardeners. *Schizostylis coccinea* makes a good gift since it increases readily by a running root system, and she was given a clump from the garden of nearby Ebor Hall. At Poleska it grew well and seeded, and about 1918 she noticed that one of the seedlings bore pink flowers instead of red.

Recognising that this was something exceptional, she isolated it. Perhaps Lady Ardilaun, a local member of the Guinness family with whom she was friendly, gave her an introduction to Sir Frederick Moore, Director of Dublin's Botanic Garden, Glasnevin. At any rate Blanche Hegarty took her pink schizostylis to Glasnevin, where Sir Frederick named it after its raiser, and persuaded her to exhibit it in London.

Plant breeders' rights did not exist in those days, but, after the stir her plant created at the Royal Horticultural Society, bulb specialists Messrs Barr and Sons made Mrs Hegarty a handsome offer for stock, and were thus the first to offer the novelty for sale.

Schizostylis coccinea 'Mrs Hegarty' has cup-shaped flowers of a good, strong pink. Its disadvantage is that flowering only begins in October and ceases with the first hard frosts, whereas pink-flowered varieties bred more recently bloom as early as August. S.c. 'Mrs Hegarty' has withstood the test of more than seventy years however, and is still widely grown.

Mrs Blanche Hegarty with her husband and younger daughter, Mrs Urquhart Dykes, the Alvis racing driver.

MISS JESSOPP
1861–c1935

Rosmarinus officinalis 'Miss Jessopp's Upright'

Miss Euphemia Jessopp was born in 1861, of a respected Enfield family. Her father was a solicitor, and until the age of fifty she kept house for her brother, a Magistrates' Clerk, and their elderly mother, at the comfortable family home of Forty Hill House. She taught in the local Sunday School and concerned herself with good works, as was expected of an Edwardian spinster. In 1911 however her brother married, and Euphemia was able to set up home locally and give full rein to her interest in gardening.

Effie, as she was known affectionately to her friends, must have been both keen and knowledgeable, for she was a gardening friend of E. A. Bowles (*qv*), and frequently visited his wonderful garden nearby. He in turn often called in to admire the alpines planted in sinks that were her special interest, and when Bowles went plant hunting in the Alps, Miss Jessopp was entrusted with the boxes of collected plants sent home.

Besides alpines, and probably planted for culinary reasons, there grew in her tiny garden a particularly upright rosemary. The likelihood is that she gave a young plant to Bowles, and he popularised it by passing on cuttings in his turn under the name, 'Miss Jessopp's Upright'.

Rosmarinus officinalis is a very variable shrub, and there are several tall, narrow forms, known variously as *R. o. pyramidalis*, *erectus* and *fastigiatus*, with little to choose between them. 'Miss Jessopp's Upright' is probably just a particularly hardy form of *R. o. fastigiatus*. With leaves of deep green above and grey beneath, it is one of the first to bloom—in a mild winter the pale blue flowers may open in January.

In the 1920's Bowles named another plant after his unassuming gardening friend. A deep blue-purple, self-coloured iris he had raised was called *Iris* 'Miss Jessopp'. It seems however to have dropped out of cultivation and never gave her the immortality of the rosemary, which is after all for remembrance.

ABBOTSWOOD AND MARK FENWICK
1861–1945

Lychnis × *walkeri* 'Abbotswood Rose'
Nerine bowdenii 'Mark Fenwick'
Potentilla fruticosa 'Abbotswood'
Rose 'Abbotswood'

Abbotswood was one of the great gardens of England in the 1930's, the creation of Mark Fenwick, a gifted and dedicated gardener. He came from a Newcastle banking family, and in 1902 bought Abbotswood, near Stow-on-the-Wold in Gloucestershire. The district was cold, and the ground afflicted by moles, pheasants and a plague of black slugs—'larger and finer and more numerous that in any other garden in England', he reported ruefully. The land however sloped to the south west, and was blessed with water in the form of three streams. Fenwick could see that it had great potential.

He engaged the architect Edwin Lutyens, then comparatively unknown. The result was a harmonious integration of remodelled house and garden, with steps and paved terraces, a parterre, ornamental pool, and three-sided outdoor 'room'.

A quantity of stone was brought in and laid to look like rocky outcrops, and streams were dammed to form two small pools, with miniature cascades and rapids. At the waterside damp-loving subjects thrived, while further up choice plants enjoyed the sheltered pockets formed by the rocks. The three small streams ran down the hill, joining under the drive to re-emerge as one.

In the Rock Garden were drifts of snowdrops, anemones, specie tulips and many choice bulbs in spring, followed by saxifrages, gentians and other treasures. Later months were not forgotten either, and in 1926 plants for interest in September and October included *Potentilla fruticosa*. This may well have been the white-flowered form which has become known as 'Abbotswood'. Thought to be a chance seedling, it not only bears flowers well into autumn, but has a fairly prostrate habit which would not look out of place in a large Rock Garden.

Mark Fenwick planted trees and shrubs lavishly, displaying

knowledge and artistry, also a rare ability to plan for their future maturity. He was keen too on autumn colour, and many of his choices were made with this in mind.

In its heyday Abbotswood enjoyed the attentions of eleven gardeners, the Head Gardener being a Mr Fred Tustin. A cantankerous individual who had been an undergardener to Lord Redesdale, he became one of the most knowledgeable and respected head gardeners of his generation. He could not abide children, a dislike heartily reciprocated by Mark Fenwick's five daughters, but the success of the garden owed much to the harmonious partnership of the two men.

Although at one in gardening aims and ideas, they did tend to differ in their willingness to give plants away. Visitors to Abbotswood were numerous, and Mark Fenwick took pleasure in seeing that few went away empty-handed. Mr Tustin did not feel quite the same, and would look on with disapproval when plants and cuttings were being given away. If instructed to send a plant on, he would often conveniently forget.

An extremely knowledgeable plantsman, Mark Fenwick served on various committees of the Royal Horticultural Society, and was a regular attender and exhibitor at its fortnightly shows, dressed in a frockcoat and top hat. He was crippled with arthritis in his later years, but, having always been keen on technology, he acquired one of the very first electric wheelchairs. In this, travelling slowly but in considerable style, he negotiated the London streets and attended RHS Shows. Uncomplaining and undaunted, he also continued to enjoy every part of Abbotswood's garden in the wheelchair, his books, labels and a few tools carried in a box behind.

'Let me say at once that only quite ordinary things can be grown here', Fenwick declared in 1926. 'I do not specialise in anything in particular, but subject to limitations of climate I grow practically everything that is worth growing in the way of hardy herbaceous and alpine plants and shrubs, which I try to plant in suitable positions'. He was too modest. With a Rose Garden, Flower Garden, Dutch Garden, orangery, pools and streams, heathers, shrubs, trees and Rock Garden, his creation was a feast for expert and casual observer alike. Visitors often claimed that there was more colour at Abbotswood than in any other garden they knew.

Lychnis × walkeri 'Abbotswood Rose' is a colourful character in any garden. Lower-growing than *Lycnis coronaria*, the silvery leaves and stalks are set off by flowers of such intense cerise that they almost shimmer, although the petals turn darker with age. At first it was thought to be a distinctive form of *Lychnis coronaria*, but research now suggests it is a hybrid between *Lychnis coronaria* and *L. flos-jovis*. Like the latter it is reliably perennial, and also comes true from seed. Mark Fenwick never seems to have mentioned or exhibited this rather special lychnis, but in 1935 it was hailed as a very good new plant, and that year Edinburgh Botanic Gardens set aside a complete bed in which to grow it.

In the 1930's there also flourished at Abbotswood a particularly fine form of the hardy *Nerine bowdenii*. The origin is unknown, but it was taller, and more floriferous than the species, the blooms being bright pink. Around 1935 when Mark Fenwick was visiting Lionel de Rothschild's great garden at Exbury, he gave five bulbs of his special nerine to the wife of Exbury's Head Gardener, Francis Hanger. Hanger was particularly interested in nerines, but grew mostly the tender varieties, whereas the one from Abbotswood was hardy.

Mrs Hanger planted the bulbs against the wall outside her dining room, and in ten years they had multiplied sufficiently to produce a good quantity of flowers. At the Royal Horticultural Society's Great Autumn Show of 1945 Francis Hanger exhibited a group of nerines, mostly his own hybrids, while his wife picked a large vaseful of her special nerine. Mark Fenwick had died just a few months earlier, and Mrs Hanger exhibited the flower as *Nerine bowdenii* 'Fenwick's Variety'. It received an Award of Merit.

The following year Francis Hanger was appointed Curator of Wisley Garden, and the bulbs were transferred to his wife's new garden. Fifteen years later, after she was widowed, they moved with her again, and in 1966 she showed the nerine once more, this time gaining a First Class Certificate. It is now known as *Nerine bowdenii* 'Mark Fenwick'. Mrs Hanger's care of the plant for over thirty years ensured its establishment as a named variety, as well as commemorating a talented gardener.

In 1946 Abbotswood was bought by a Mr and Mrs Harry Ferguson, who continued the garden's development, opening up bigger vistas, planting new areas of trees and rhododendrons, and bulldozing a lake. The garden was restored after wartime neglect, and immaculately kept. For the first years, they were fortunate in retaining the services of the formidable Fred Tustin, and in 1954 he noticed a rather special dog rose had seeded itself into the hedge surrounding the kitchen garden. Its pink, sweetly-scented flowers were semi-double. Fred pointed it out to Graham Thomas, the shrub rose enthusiast, who propagated it and put it on the market, naming it 'Abbotswood'.

Tustin was succeeded by a talented Scotsman, Andrew Blakeley, who contributed much to the garden in his turn. Mr Ferguson died in 1960, and although his widow continued to devote herself to the garden, it was too labour-intensive to be easy to keep. Abbotswood was sold a few years later, after her death, and is now open in the spring under the National Gardens Scheme.

Nerine bowdenii 'Mark Fenwick'

SIR ARTHUR HORT
1864–1935

Globularia meridionalis 'Hort's Variety'
Lychnis flos-jovis 'Hort's Variety'

Many gardeners regard the Latin names of plants as something of a barrier, but Sir Arthur Hort delighted in them and could be relied on to explain a plant's classical background or ancient association. He was a rare blend of lofty intellect and sensible practicality, who found in gardening lasting pleasure and satisfaction.

The son of a gardening parson who was an expert on the genus Rubus, Arthur inherited an instinctive feeling for plants. He was also imbued with an enthusiasm for the classics, which, after Cambridge, he went on to teach at Harrow School. There he had an old walled garden where his love of iris was particularly indulged, and in due course Hort retired to The Old Rectory at Hurstbourne Tarrant in Hampshire.

The new garden consisted of two steeply sloping acres on uncompromisingly chalk soil. 'I hold that the gardener, unless he is in a position to 'manure his garden with banknotes' should take his soil as he finds it, and grow therein the plants which like it', Hort declared, but the range of plants he managed to cultivate there was enormous.

On his many botanising trips, plants were collected from places as far apart as Corsica and the Alps, Ireland and the Pyrenees. He contributed gardening articles to the Guardian newspaper, which were spiced with modesty and humour, and he made it a rule only to write about plants that he had grown himself. Even with this stricture the two books he published about his garden and its occupants reveal encyclopaedic knowledge—'jottings from my own experience', he called them diffidently.

The ordinary, magenta, and rather untidy form of *Lychnis flos-jovis*, Hort reckoned was fit only for the wild garden. But on one alpine foray he came across a much more desirable form. Growing high on the slopes of Mont Cernis, there was 'a dwarfer, smarter form with the same grey, flannelly leaves, but short-stemmed heads of a beautiful, lucent pink. It grew in the tangle of a luxuriant meadow among geranium and trollius', he reported, 'and is (to judge by numerous requests for seed) a quite excellent plant for rockery or front of border.' Many alpines dislike our maritime climate, but *Lychnis flos-jovis* 'Hort's Variety' is only unhappy in boggy soil. Putting down long roots, it will tolerate poor soil and dry conditions without distress, and produces so much seed that the great number of gardeners who now grow it is hardly surprising.

A dry, hot place is essential for the other plant which bears Hort's name. 'Globularias may not appeal to those who insist on brilliant colouring', he observed, 'but in their neat quiet way they have a fascination'. Low-growing rock plants, globularias have little flowers resembling furry, blue globes, and Hort grew several different sorts, most of which he had collected himself. After visiting the Pyrenees one summer, he recorded, 'I dug up by happy chance another species which at the time I somehow failed to recognise as distinct.' The plant made a tight hump a few inches across, and Kew botanists eventually identified it as a good form of *Globularia bellidifolia*, meaning "daisy-leaved"', (now changed to *G. meridionalis*). 'It is a jewel of a plant to propagate', Hort remarked, 'you can pull it to pieces like a primrose, and every piece will have some fibrous roots attached.' The find took well to his dry Hampshire garden, and later he was pleased to record that his globularia had found its way into many rock-gardens, including that of Kew.

Five decades on, Hort's globularia is not often encountered, but the Lychnis which commemorates this scholarly gardener continues to be widely grown.

LANARTH AND
P. D. WILLIAMS
1865–1935

Erica vagans alba 'St Keverne'
Erica × *williamsii* 'P. D. Williams'
Magnolia campbellii mollicomata 'Lanarth'
Narcissus 'Lanarth'
Rhododendron 'Mrs P. D. Williams'
Rhododendron 'St Keverne'
Viburnum plicatum 'Lanarth'

Lanarth, situated near the Helford River in Cornwall, was for forty-two years the home of Percival Dacres Williams, universally known as P. D. The estate had been bought by his father as a shooting box, but in 1893, aged 28, P. D. and his unmarried sister moved in, and he began planting a wonderful garden.

Gardening was in the family's blood, his cousin was J. C. Williams of Caerhays Castle, who was also to make a major contribution to horticulture, and the two corresponded almost daily about happenings in their respective gardens.

P. D. also kept a Garden Book at Lanarth, and in its first entry in 1896 recorded the planting of various trees and shrubs, including 'half a dozen *Viburnum plicatum*'. The garden was blessed with a rich soil and in its mild climate most things grew well. However these viburnums became exceptionally large. When mature, each measured some 15ft × 15ft (4.6m × 4.6m), presenting a fine sight in early summer with their horizontal branches covered in flat, creamy blooms. In 1926 Mr W. J. Bean, the leading authority on shrubs and trees, visited the garden seeking specimens for Kew. One of the things he noted as desirable was '*Viburnum tomentosum* (Lanarth form—very large and impressive)'. Four years later it was exhibited by a friend of P. D's, Lionel de Rothschild of Exbury. The species' botanical name has now reverted to *V. plicatum*, after being argued over for years, and *V. p.* 'Lanarth' has remained a popular shrub despite the trend to smaller gardens.

It was not surprising that Rothschild was a gardening friend, for both he and P. D. were rhododendron enthusiasts. The collection at

Lanarth was considered one of the best in England, and Williams enjoyed breeding his own. Red-flowered *Rhododendron* 'St Keverne', named after the nearby village, was exhibited at Chelsea in 1922. *Rhododendron*, 'Mrs P. D. Williams', however, did not come from Lanarth. It was a promising new seedling bred by Knapp Hill Nursery of Surrey, who named it to please a good customer.

P. D. Williams was interested in daffodils from the start, making his first cross in 1895. Over the next forty years he was responsible for producing numerous good varieties. One expert declared that it is impossible to visualise the present day family of hybrid narcissi without the flowers Williams bred. He was particularly attracted by the shallow-crowned 'Jonquil' type, and the one he named 'Lanarth' is a very good form, having a golden yellow perianth and neat little cup of coppery yellow, tinged with orange. Springtime in his garden was breathtaking, with great drifts of narcissus among the thick plantings of trees and shrubs.

One of the highlights of early spring at Lanarth, however, its creator never lived to see. Just a year or so before he died P. D. planted a young *Magnolia campbellii mollicomata*, raised from seed brought back from the Yunnan by another friend, the plant collector George Forrest. This tree takes about fifteen years to flower, and the one at Lanarth first produced its rich violet-purple cups in 1947. That year P. D's son Michael exhibited flowering branches, and it was given the variety name of 'Lanarth'. Reputedly the earliest magnolia to flower in Cornwall, this magnificent tree is considered by some to be the most beautiful that has ever come out of China.

P. D. Williams had a wide circle of friends and interests. He carried out duties as a magistrate, sat on Royal Horticultural Society and local committees, and at the age of 38 became High Sheriff of Cornwall, yet he still found time to enjoy the lovely countryside around Lanarth. In October 1910 he was able to record in the Garden Book, 'I found in Trelan Valley a distinct hybrid Heath'. A bushy plant, about 2ft 6 in (76cm) high, the flowers were orchid purple, and botanists declared it to be a hybrid between *Erica tetralix* and *E. vagans*. P. D. was not, however, the first to discover this heather. Strangely enough, in the mid-nineteenth century it had been noted in the same place by P. D's uncle, but no record of the find had been published. Thus the new plant became *Erica* × *williamsii* 'P. D. Williams'.

A year after this rediscovery P. D. was out walking in August

68

when his eye was caught by another interesting heather. 'I today found a white form of *Erica vagans* with creamy anthers, not crimson as usual', he wrote, and in due course this became *Erica vagans alba* 'St Keverne'.

Williams not only had an observant eye, but a talent for grouping plants together, and he was not afraid of thinning and pruning boldly to create the effects he wanted. Thus it must have been a terrible blow to lose most of his sight in his late sixties, but instead of being embittered he made light of the affliction. 'I see character of form and no longer beauty around me', he wrote to a friend. 'But at my age it is a good thing to be automatically relieved of some portion of one's ever increasing work.'

After his death in 1935 the Royal Horticultural Society set up a memorial fund to provide awards, to be known as P. D. Williams Medals. Since daffodils and rhododendrons were his own special interests, the medals bearing his name are awarded for outstanding daffodil and rhododendron exhibits, in alternate years.

Lanarth – 'Early spring at Lanarth. The tree is the Japanese, summer-flowering *Magnolia hypoleuca*'.

E. A. BOWLES
1865–1954

Anemone japonica 'Bowles' Pink'
Carex stricta 'Bowles' Golden'
Colchicum 'E. A. Bowles'
Crocus chrysanthus 'E. A. Bowles'
Crocus sieberi 'Bowles' White'
Cyclamen hederifolium 'Bowles' Apollo Strain'
Daphne mezereum 'Bowles' Variety'
Erysimum linifolium 'Bowles' Mauve'
Hebe 'Bowles' Hybrid'
Hebe 'E. A. Bowles'
Iris germanica 'Myddelton Blue'
Lavandula 'Bowles' Variety'
Mentha rotundifolia 'Bowles'
Milium effusum aureum, 'Bowles' Golden Grass'
Oxalis 'Bowles' White'
Penstemon 'Myddelton Gem'
Phlomis fruticosa 'Edward Bowles'
Pulmonaria 'Bowles' Red'
Ranunculus ficaria 'Bowles' Double'
Rheum palmatum 'Bowles' Crimson'
Salix 'Bowles' Hybrid'
Skimmia japonica 'Bowles' Dwarf'
Vinca minor 'Bowles' Variety'
Viola 'Bowles' Black'

Edward Augustus Bowles was probably the greatest amateur gardener of his time. Scholarly, dedicated, warm, humorous and philanthropic, he was certainly one of the most loved.

The third son of a prosperous Enfield family, E. A. Bowles was destined for the Church after leaving Cambridge University, but family bereavement caused him instead to go back to live with his parents. He had an enquiring and scientific mind and was first interested in entymology. Whilst at Cambridge he would go on moth and caterpillar hunting expeditions to nearby Wicken Fen, and it was here that he discovered what became known as 'Bowles' Golden Sedge', the first plant to bear his name. In a clump of *Carex stricta*, a sedge with ordinary green leaves, he noticed two or three shoots banded with pure yellow. With his pocket knife he severed this portion and took it back to his parents' garden at Myddelton House where it flourished, later to become a much-coveted plant.

Gardening soon grew into an absorbing interest—'collecting plants and endeavouring to keep them alive', he called it—and his father tolerantly allowed his energetic son a free hand with the riverside garden at Myddelton House. It had been dull and Victorian in style, with bedding plants and spotted laurels, but over the years was transformed into a spectacular 'plantsman's garden', a Mecca both for keen gardeners and for the many local boys to whom 'Uncle G' was friend and benefactor.

E. A. Bowles did not just seek beauty in the plants he grew, he had a wry and mischievous humour and appreciated quirkiness in nature. A corner of the garden became a 'home for demented plants' such as the madly twisting Corkscrew Hazel, *Corylus avellan* 'Contorta', *Plantago major* 'Rosularis' which has extra leaves instead of flowers, a pigmy elder and many more. He called the area his Lunatic Asylum.

Bowles suffered from hay fever, and this gave him an excellent excuse for departing regularly in June to the Alps, plant hunting with various friends. These trips enhanced not only his knowledge but his understanding of alpines, and the conditions they liked, and he established a rock garden at Myddelton which became home to an astonishing range of plants.

In 1914, returning home through France after an alpine visit, the party paused at the church of Le Grav. Bowles wandered round the churchyard and was very taken with the glossy leaves of a periwinkle growing there. He brought a few runners home, and next year the find proved to have beautiful blue flowers. Amos Perry (*qv*), a friend and local nurseryman, soon grew it commercially and called it *Vinca minor* 'Bowles' Variety'. The plant was a commercial success, and became popular in America for planting on graves.

A good number of Bowles' plants became well known through Amos Perry. The nurseryman was given numerous plants from Myddelton, and also named many new introductions in Bowles' honour, as did others in the trade. In 1901 Perry's Hardy Plant Farm launched a little black viola, now a sought after plant among keen gardeners, seeds of which had come to Myddelton House garden from a friend. Perry called it *Viola* Bowles' Black', a name which Bowles disliked, but not as much as Viola 'Black Bowles', a label spotted by the flower's namesake at a subsequent Chelsea Flower Show. He quietly altered it.

A modest and unassuming man, E. A. Bowles would have been drily amused at the number of plants now named after him, many of them spuriously. He had an eye for good plants however, and exchanged visits, seeds and cuttings with almost all the great gardeners of his day. He was also unfailingly generous with material from his own garden, his habitual greeting to visitors being, 'I hope you've brought a basket with you'. When in their turn recipients passed on those plants it would be with a proud comment such as, 'This is E. A. Bowles' pulmonaria'. So the number of 'Bowles' plants is perhaps not surprising.

Several of the most famous plants raised by him do not actually bear his name. Crocuses were a great passion, and he selected some very good seedlings of *Crocus chrysanthus*, calling them after birds. *C. chrysanthus* 'Siskin' and 'Yellowhammer' are not much heard of some seventy years on, but *C. chrysanthus* 'Snow Bunting' is now probably the most widely sold of all the early crocuses. The appropriately named, pale blue *Iris reticulata* 'Cantab' we also owe to Bowles' sharp eye for an outstanding seedling.

Besides collecting plants and receiving seeds and cuttings from his many friends, Bowles begged a number of plants that caught his eye in cottage gardens. One day when he and a friend had a day out moth-hunting and ended up hungry and miles from anywhere, they went to a cottage and asked if they could have a meal. The woman of the house gave them lamb, with mint sauce so good that Bowles remarked on it. 'Oh that's the lamb mint', she said, and showed him a furry-leaved variety of *Mentha rotundifolia*. She gave him some roots to take home, and as he in turn gave it away it became a 'Bowles' plant.

Curiously, the most well-known of the plants that bear his name, *Erysimum linifolium* 'Bowles' Mauve', he almost certainly never grew. This shrubby wallflower is spectacularly different from other forms in its strong mauve colour, and it blooms from February through to autumn. Bowles wrote several highly successful books, including three which described his garden through the seasons, yet he never mentioned this wallflower. After Bowles' death Frances Perry, Amos's daughter-in-law, who had known Myddelton House garden from childhood, showed the wallflower to the men who had worked in the garden. They had never seen it before. It is undoubtedly the sort of plant Bowles would have liked, but its origin and why his name was linked to it remains a mystery.

Another very popular 'Bowles' plant is *Milium effusum aureum*, 'Bowles' Golden Grass', which he acquired from Birmingham Botanic Garden. 'A wonderful grass', Bowles remarked, 'with the lightest, clearest yellow of any leaf I know, a veritable treasure'.

Myddelton House garden was full of such treasures and, with his scholarly mind, artistic flair and devotion to plants, Edward Bowles was undoubtedly the most knowledgeable plantsman of his generation. He was however endearingly modest. 'My garden is too big for its boots', he once commented dismissively, 'aping its betters in attempting to grow far too many plants that are unsuitable for its harsh climate and shallow soil'. The President of the Royal Horticultural Society echoed the opinion of most visitors however, when he wrote, 'It is doubtful whether there ever was a garden more packed with choice and beautiful plants'.

A life Fellow of the Royal Horticultural Society, and recipient of its highest honours, Bowles served on many of its committees right up until his death in 1954, despite failing health and eventual blindness.

Never having married, in old age the fate of his beloved garden worried him, but Bowles was pleased when the University of London's School of Pharmacy agreed to take it on as a home for the study of the active properties of plants. This prevented the land from being built over, but inevitably the garden as created and planted by Bowles did not long survive. The house and most of the grounds were eventually sold to the Lee Valley Park Authority, the garden became overgrown, and it is only in the last few years that work has begun to reverse the years of neglect.

After Bowles' death the Royal Horticultural Society set aside a corner of their garden at Wisley in honour of this outstanding gardener and much-loved man. Bowles' Corner consists of over 150 plants, shrubs and trees, all of which he grew at Myddelton. No fewer than seventeen bear his name. As a great plantsman it would surely please E. A. Bowles that plants are his enduring memorial.

ELSTEAD NURSERY AND ERNEST LADHAMS
1867–1952

Carpenteria californica 'Ladhams' Variety'
Cimicifuga simplex 'Elstead Variety'
Cotoneaster salicifolius 'Elstead'
Erigeron glaucus 'Elstead Pink'
Hypericum inodorum 'Elstead Variety'
Veronica 'Shirley Blue'

E lstead, a village near Godalming in Surrey, was for twenty years the home of Ernest Ladhams, whose nursery there became renowned for good plants in the 1930's.

The Ladhams family already had a thriving 90-acre nursery at Shirley, Southampton, started about 1870 by Ernest's father Benjamin. The business sold cut flowers, soft fruit, seeds, roses and a few hardy plants, but when Ernest and his brother Charles took control they began to grow many more perennials.

Erigeron 'B Ladhams' (named after old Benjamin), *Lobelia* 'Shirley Beauty' and many more were produced, and are now mostly forgotten, but the large-flowered *Veronica* 'Shirley Blue' had star quality. 'Leaves all previous blues quite behind', Ladhams announced proudly, and many decades later it is still an extraordinarily good herbaceous plant.

Although the nursery grew mostly border plants they did stock *Carpenteria californica*, a somewhat tender shrub with narrow leaves and white, philadelphus-like flowers in summer. It is rather variable from seed, and so is generally reproduced by cuttings. In 1924 Ladhams offered a variety, propagated from a sport, which they called *Carpenteria californica grandiflora*. It had flowers that were 'large white, as opposed to white', and for this novelty customers had to pay seven shillings and sixpence, instead of five shillings. Later it became known as *C.c.* 'Ladhams' Variety', and anyone who has seen a bush in full flower will know that the extra half a crown was well spent. Its dazzling white flowers are often over 3in (7.5cm) across, and produced in such profusion that the effect is spectacular.

Ladhams of Southampton closed in 1935 on the death of Charles Ladhams, but Ernest had left three years earlier and gone to live with his wife and daughter at Elstead. Although nearly sixty, he acquired some thirty acres of land, and started a nursery which concentrated on hardy perennials. The soil was almost pure sand, but he found that by double-trenching almost anything would grow. One of his specialities was raising pinks from seed, a whole acre being devoted to them. He listed thirty different varieties, but none of his 'Elstead strain' now remain, nor the delphiniums, violas, primulas and almost all the other border plants which bore the name 'Elstead'.

Cimicifuga simplex 'Elstead Variety' has however become a classic plant for moist soil. This cimicifuga normally has green leaves, and in early Autumn long-stalked, white flowers arch upwards like elegant bottle-brushes. By careful breeding, Ernest Ladhams succeeded in producing a shorter form, with purplish flower stems, and mauve-tinted buds. He introduced his new plant in 1932, and it was soon much in demand.

Ernest Ladhams was fascinated by plant breeding and had a reputation in the trade as a very skilled propagator. Most of his introductions were grown from seed, and although many featured only minor improvements, like *Cotoneaster salicifolius* 'Elstead' which has rich coppery leaves in autumn, a few were distinctive. *Hypericum inodorum* 'Elstead' was one such. Instead of the normal black fruits, Ladham's hypericum has attractive red berries, and the shrub displays flowers and berries at the same time. Nowadays *H.i.* 'Elstead' is so widely grown that it is difficult to find the original species.

Erigerons were a particular interest. For a long time *Erigeron* 'B Ladhams' was popular, being one of the first to feature orange buds, but modern nurserymen have ceased to grow it. The only Ladhams' erigeron that remains commercially available is the lilac-tinted *Erigeron glaucus* 'Elstead Pink', dating from the nursery's early years.

The stream of new plants from Elstead continued throughout the Thirties, exhibits at Chelsea and other shows drew much praise and comment, and its reputation grew. But the business was labour intensive, and when war broke out Ernest Ladhams was faced with a drastic drop in orders and virtually no labour. Much of the stock had to be destroyed, which nearly broke his heart, although the nursery struggled on through the war. Ladhams' wife died, and in

1946 he sold up and went to live in Jamaica where he himself died six years later.

The business did not long survive, and nowadays there is a housing estate on the site of what was once the famous Elstead nursery.

Carpenteria californica 'Ladhams' Variety'

VISCOUNTESS BYNG OF VIMY
1870–1949

Primula allionii 'Viscountess Byng'
Schizostylis coccinea 'Viscountess Byng'

In 1913 General and Lady Byng bought a house at Thorpe le
Soken in North Essex, after years serving in South Africa and
Egypt. Estate agents, it seems, have always had trouble with reality.
Thorpe Hall had been advertised as 'a stately Georgian mansion in
spacious gardens with magnificent timber and a fine sheet of ornamental water'. Lady Byng reported wryly that it was actually a
derelict, square, white house, screaming for a coat of paint or
plaster. The 'spacious garden' was a jungle of untrimmed laurels, a
sea of nettles and docks, and the lake so thickly covered with slimy
green weed that you could hardly tell where the grass ended and
water began. Lady Byng was a keen gardener, however, and saw in
it great possibilities.

During the First World War the house was turned into a thirty-
bed hospital, so that only in 1918 were the Byngs able to begin
remodelling both house and garden. Gradually the twelve acres
were tamed, terraces were created, together with a sunken garden,
and special areas for alpines, roses, irises and moisture-loving
plants.

General Byng served with distinction in the 1914–18 war, and
four years later was appointed Governor General of Canada.
Instead of complaining about being separated from her garden,
Lady Evelyn took the opportunity whenever she could to go plant
hunting in Canada, the West Indies and California. She revelled in
the wild vastness of California after the formality of Ottawa's
Government House, but remarked laughingly, 'Walking is an in-
comprehensible thing to the average American, and to their way of
thinking you walk either because you have not got a car or because
you are a mildly mental case'.

Returning to Thorpe Hall in 1926, now Viscountess Byng of
Vimy, she began exhibiting her best plants at the Royal Horticultural Society's fortnightly shows. Alpines were a particular

enthusiasm and she was probably a good customer of Six Hills Nursery (*qv*) which specialised in alpines. At any rate when Frank Barker of Six Hills produced an award-winning seedling of *Primula allionii* just before the Second World War, he named it 'Viscountess Byng'. The flowers are rose pink with a small white eye, and broad, rounded petals, each with a notch at the end.

Vivacious, enthusiastic and hospitable, with a wide circle of gardening friends, including E. A. Bowles (*qv*), and Queen Mary, a regular visitor, Lady Byng enjoyed both receiving and giving choice plants. 'Gardening is the only occupation or profession I know of in which the layman and professional meet on a common ground in a common cause, and are willing, almost always, to help one another', she once observed.

To Amos Perry (*qv*), proprietor of Perry's Hardy Plant Farm at Enfield, she was both customer and gardening friend, and he named after her a promising new variety of the Kaffir Lily, *Schizostylis coccinea*. The first pink-flowered form, *S.c.* 'Mrs Hegarty' (*qv*), had been introduced in 1921, but a few years later Perry produced another pink form, *Schizostylis coccinea* 'Viscountess Byng'. In his catalogue he extolled it as, 'a very charming introduction, totally distinct, with a vigorous habit, stout spikes well furnished with large, open flowers. Delightful shade of soft rose—two shillings and sixpence each'.

He might have added that, being very late-flowering, *S.c.* 'Viscountess Byng' is often cut down by frost while still in her youth, and is sometimes shy about producing her delicate blooms at all. Lady Byng herself certainly found this, recording that in her garden the plant produced 'a forest of leaves but no flowers, which in the circumstances seems unfriendly'.

She did not comment about the performance of a day lily which Amos Perry had also named in her honour, but he had no doubt that it was outstanding. *Hemerocallis* 'Viscountess Byng', he advertised, gave flowers 7in (17cm) across, 'in a striking shade of dark terracotta overlaid bronze, with a deep orange base', and for just one plant customers had to part with twenty-one shillings.

Perhaps the high price discouraged purchasers, but *Hemerocallis* 'Viscountess Byng' soon faded from the scene and is no longer available, whereas the delicate pink schizostylis remains a firm favourite.

HIDCOTE AND LAWRENCE JOHNSTON
1871–1958

Campanula latiloba 'Hidcote Amethyst'
Dianthus 'Hidcote'
Fuchsia 'Hidcote Beauty'
Hypericum 'Hidcote'
Lavandula angustifolia 'Hidcote'
Lavandula angustifolia 'Hidcote Pink'
Lavandula × intermedia 'Hidcote Giant'
Penstemon 'Hidcote Pink'
Rose 'Hidcote Gold'
Rose 'Lawrence Johnston'
Symphytum grandiflorum 'Hidcote Blue'
Symphytum grandiflorum 'Hidcote Pink'
Verbena 'Hidcote Purple'
Verbena 'Lawrence Johnston'

Garden visiting has become such a popular pastime that many thousands of people now flock annually to the garden of Hidcote Bartrim Manor, deep in the Gloucestershire countryside. A delightful blend of formality with natural planting, and acknowledged as one of our greatest gardens. Hidcote was the creation of a quiet, reticent American, Lawrence Johnston.

The eldest son of a well-to-do banker, Lawrence was born in France, where he spent his earliest years. He took a degree in History at Cambridge University, and later became a naturalised British citizen.

When Lawrence was a teenager, his younger brother and father died, and his mother, Gertrude, married a lawyer named Charles Winthrop. Only eleven years later Gertrude was left a widow for the second time, with the result that Lawrence became the sole object of his mother's rather stifling devotion. The advent of the Boer War, however, gave him an opportunity to enjoy a little independence, and he joined the British Army.

After the Boer war Johnston tried his hand at farming, and in 1907 Gertrude bought the estate of Hidcote Bartrim, which included 300 acres of land, seven cottages and the manor house.

There was no garden to speak of, but before long the farm was put in the care of a manager, and her artistic son was enthusiastically planning a garden that used the hilltop site with flair and imagination. His ambitious designs owed much to the disciplined restraint of continental gardens with which he was familiar, but he also numbered among his friends Norah Lindsay, a garden designer who advocated exuberant and colourful planting.

The outbreak of the First World War in 1914 halted the development of Hidcote's garden. Lawrence Johnston, now a Major, was seriously wounded in the fighting. When peace came, he returned to Hidcote, threw himself whole-heartedly into reversing the neglect of the war years, and designed yet more ambitious schemes.

The garden was divided into about a dozen separate areas, each differing in theme and atmosphere. 'Mrs Winthrop's Garden' was planted with flowers of blue and yellow, his mother's favourite colours; the 'Stream Garden' had crowded, naturalistic planting beside a winding path; and hornbeams clipped to form hedges at head height became 'The Stilt Garden'. Johnston furnished his garden 'rooms' so that they looked their best at different times of the year, the aesthetically pleasing designs showing off his clever plant associations to perfection. Even in its early days a visitor to Hidcote was moved to comment, 'This man is planting his garden as no-one else has ever planted a garden.'

All this took an ever-increasing amount of money, and it was Gertrude Winthrop who held the purse-strings. When Johnston conceived a new scheme for the garden, to him money was no object, but his mother despaired of the endless spending, and relations were often strained as a result.

Mrs Winthrop was becoming frail, and Lawrence Johnston himself did not enjoy good health, so in 1924, two years before she died, he bought a villa at Menton, near Monte Carlo, where they could escape the English winter. Naturally he soon embarked on making a remarkable garden there too, and the mild climate meant that he could grow a greater range of plants than at Hidcote.

Johnston was a naturally brilliant garden designer, but initially, not particularly knowledgeable about plants. Before long, however, he had developed a wide circle of gardening friends, and in 1927 joined Collingwood Ingram (*qv*) and two others in a plant-hunting expedition to South and East Africa. Ingram remarked that 'Johnny' enjoyed his luxuries—his valet and cook went with them, and whenever possible they travelled in his chauffeur-driven car.

Four years later Johnston joined the plant explorer George Forrest on a more gruelling trip to Yunnan, in Western China. Some of the plants that returned with him were given to the Edinburgh Botanic Garden, or to gardening friends, but many were planted at Hidcote or Menton.

Rosa sericea pteracantha comes from that part of China, and Johnston probably brought back a specimen. It is most often white-flowered, with prominent thorns, but the vigorous specimen now named 'Hidcote Gold' bears graceful sprays of five-petalled, yellow flowers. Wild specimens are occasionally yellow-flowered, and it may be from original seed, or a hybrid with a yellow rose such as *R. hugonis*.

Johnston's eye for a good plant gave future gardeners a much more popular rose. At the turn of the century yellow garden roses suitable for cool climates were the great quest of rose breeders. The Persian yellow rose, *Rosa foetida*, proved almost impossible to breed from, but Joseph Pernet-Ducher of Lyons kept trying longer than most. Persistance and a bit of luck eventually gave him first an orangey rose, and later a pure yellow named 'Rayon d'Or', which he launched in 1910. Breeding continued, and in 1923 came 'La Rêve', a yellow climber, the result of a cross between the Persian rose and one called 'Madame Eugene Verdier'. Another seedling grew from this cross, but Pernet-Ducher rejected it as not worthy of introduction, and simply left it to grow on, unnamed.

On his journeys between Gloucestershire and the South of France Lawrence Johnston probably made a point of visiting the famous Lyons nursery. This poorly regarded yellow rose must have caught his eye, for it came back with him to Hidcote. Planted against a wall in what is now known as 'The Old Garden', the rose produced an abundance of semi-double, scented, warm yellow flowers, and was much admired, becoming known as 'Hidcote Yellow'. In 1948 when it was eventually put on the market commercially, the name was changed to 'Lawrence Johnston', and the rose is now considered to be one of the best yellow climbers.

Lawrence Johnston was a very unassuming and private man, but he was happy to talk gardening with other enthusiasts, and generous with plants they admired. In 1938 Charles Raffill of Kew Gardens visited Menton, and remarked on a particularly splendid red verbena. He was given a piece, and passed the plant on to various gardens under the name *Verbena* 'Lawrence Johnston'. In 1948 it happened to be planted in a mass display in front of the Curator's

House at Wisley, prompting so many enquiries that it was declared the most popular plant of the year. Easy to grow from cuttings, this verbena with its large heads of scarlet flowers borne from June to October has remained a favourite, and is now a regular feature of the Red Borders at Hidcote.

One of the most famous plants to bear the garden's name is *Lavandula angustifolia* 'Hidcote', but its origin is obscure. Probably it was a seedling raised at Hidcote or perhaps Menton, lavenders being natives of Southern Europe. Neat in habit, and with blooms of a dark, pleasing purple, *L. a.* 'Hidcote' has a long flowering season and is so easy to grow that its popularity is unsurprising.

Carliles of Twyford (*qv*) were the first to introduce this lavender commercially, gaining permission to call it 'Hidcote' from an elderly and somewhat querulous Lawrence Johnston, who was invited to tea to discuss the matter. Accompanied by his chauffeur and secretary, he insisted on speaking French throughout but everything was settled satisfactorily, and *L. a.* 'Hidcote' has since become one of the most widely grown lavenders. Another, *Lavandula angustifolia* 'Hidcote Pink' has flowers of a delicate, greyish-pink, but there is little to choose between it and other pink forms.

In 1948 a shrubby hypericum was found growing at Hidcote which mystified botanists. Some 6 ft (2m) high and broad, semi-evergreen, and covered from July to October with large, saucer-shaped golden flowers, it was hardy, and would grow vigorously in full sun or in shade. This wonderful shrub became known as *Hypericum* 'Hidcote', and is now thought to be a hybrid between *H. calycinum*, the Rose of Sharon, and a taller, bushy hybrid named *Hypericum* 'Gold Cup'. The new shrub was exhibited in 1950 as *Hypericum* 'Hidcote', since when its vigour, hardiness and long flowering season have made it immensely popular.

Major Johnston never married, and as he became increasingly frail and lived more and more in Southern France, the fate of his remarkable creation at Hidcote worried friends. The National Trust was eventually persuaded to take it on, and in 1948 he signed a Deed of Gift giving them the house and garden. Johnston died at Menton ten years later, aged 87. He would be astounded, and probably horrified, at the number of visitors who now throng Hidcote garden on a summer afternoon, but no garden designer could have a more splendid memorial.

AMOS PERRY
1871–1953

Achillea ptarmica 'Perry's White'
Aster novi-belgii 'Perry's White'
Iris sibirica 'Mrs Perry'
Iris sibirica 'Perry's Blue'
Papaver orientale 'Marcus Perry'
Papaver orientale 'Mrs Perry'
Papaver orientale 'Perry's White'

Amos Perry was born in 1871, and after leaving school joined the nursery of Thomas Ware, Tottenham, where his father was a partner. In due course he became their Bulb Foreman, and in 1893 started his own nursery at Winchmore Hill, North London. 'Perry's Hardy Plant Farm' prospered, his father joined him three years later, and the nursery moved to Enfield in order to expand.

Hardy plants were not much esteemed at that time—it was considered a concession to find space for them at any London exhibition. But when Amos Perry exhibited he did nothing by halves. In 1910 he caused a sensation by arranging 25,000 cut spikes of delphiniums in one exhibit. He grew more than 50,000 delphiniums at Enfield, and lilies, Michaelmas daisies, spiraeas and other popular border plants by the acre.

The nursery was famous for developing and introducing new varieties—one visitor marvelled at seeing 16,000 seedling irises and 8,000 hybrids of *Lilium candidum*. Obviously new varieties were good for business, but Amos Perry bred them just as much for pleasure as for profit. 'Cross-breeding, resulting in flowers totally distinct from either of its parents, is a delight which has no equal', he declared. 'The interest and pleasure transcend financial gain'.

Achillea ptarmica 'Perry's White', introduced in 1912, was a striking new plant for the garden, and greeted with excitement by the cut-flower trade. About 30 in (76cm) high, on stiff, branching stems, its white blooms are about twice the size of other double-flowered forms, and it flowers from June until late autumn.

The new cultivar was a resounding success, and Amos Perry was able to record, 'Of all the interesting perennials it has been my fortune to introduce, none has given such universal satisfaction as this, especially for cutting purposes. Its fame has spread to the four corners of the horticultural world.'

Ironically Perry's plant is only stocked nowadays by a handful of nurseries, while the smaller-flowered *Achillea ptarmica* 'The Pearl' is widely available.

Another white flower of his, which in 1920 was acclaimed by the gardening press, is now hardly seen. *Aster novi-belgii* 'Perry's White' is a single-flowered, pure white Michaelmas daisy. With a neat, erect habit, and pretty, loose petals reminiscent of a Japanese chrysanthemum, it is quite distinct. 'We have seen nothing half so good in size, floriferousness or purity', declared The Garden magazine the year it was launched.

Perry's Hardy Plant Farm was unique. Besides raising new varieties himself, Amos travelled widely in Europe to private as well as Botanic Gardens, and found many a good plant tucked away in a most unlikely corner. As a result his nursery had one of the most complete collections of hardy plants that has ever been made.

Perry also specialised in hardy ferns and aquatics. Thousands of ferns were housed in specially built, lattice-work sheds which gave just the right amount of shade. In order to grow pond and bog plants the irrigation system was designed so that parts of the nursery could be flooded, and in 1902 he staged the very first Water Garden Exhibit in this country. Subsequently his daughter-in-law, Frances Perry, did much to expand this side of the business. Her book on water gardening is still the standard work on the subject, and she became a much-respected gardening personality and writer.

Amos and his wife Nancy had four daughters and two sons, so a fair number of the nursery's new plants were named after members of the Perry family. Others honoured gardening friends or customers. With so many introductions to name however, in later years they coined the name 'Perfield', a combination of 'Perry' and 'Enfield' which sounded like a surname, e.g. *Linum narbonense* 'June Perfield'.

Having been Bulb Foreman at Thomas Ware, it is not surprising that bulbous plants were one of Amos's particular interests. He went on breeding day lilies until his death, and won much acclaim for new irises. *Iris sibirica* 'Perry's Blue', developed in 1917, remains the best sky-blue, and is still available, along with *I.s.* 'Mrs Perry', a pretty shade of rosy-white. But of all the herbaceous plants, he will probably be best remembered for his work on oriental poppies. 'In the poppy world he is a veritable king', wrote a contemporary, 'no grower can touch him'.

Plant breeders need patience and dedication in equal measure, but a little luck comes in useful. In 1903 an orangey-pink bloom appeared unexpectedly in a bed of the normally scarlet oriental poppies. Three years later Amos had sufficient numbers of it to launch it as *Papaver orientale* 'Mrs Perry'. There was great acclaim for the new colour break, but Perry was now fired with the daunting ambition to breed a white one.

In the following years patiently he crossed the palest seedlings, but success eluded him. And then he received a letter from a disgruntled customer complaining that instead of Papaver orientale 'Mrs Perry' which he had ordered for a pink border, 'a nasty fat white one had appeared'. Perry thought it must be an annual poppy, and said so, only to receive a still more irate letter saying the writer knew an annual poppy from an oriental poppy, and what did Mr Perry intend to do about it? To placate him Perry travelled to the garden, and there indeed was the long sought after white-flowered oriental poppy, which in 1912 became *Papaver orientale* 'Perry's White'. 'His giant white oriental poppy is the greatest acquisition a herbaceous border can have', enthused one gardening writer, 'and no garden of note is perfect without it'.

Amos's two sons, Gerald and Reginald, joined the business, and the tall, vivid red *Papaver orientale* 'Marcus Perry' is named after the son of Gerald and Frances, who was tragically killed in a road accident. The nursery itself did not long survive the war. Amos, affectionately known as 'the Guv'nor', retired in 1945, leaving the business to his two sons. But just a year or so later the land was compulsorily purchased, at agricultural rates, for council house building. It was a sad end to a great nursery which over half a century had achieved a world-wide reputation for herbaceous and aquatic plants.

During those years Perry's Hardy Plant Farm had introduced over 400 new cultivars and varieties. It is a pity that so few are available today, bearing in mind a comment from the editor of Gardening Illustrated—'Discerning gardeners have come to know that if a plant is 'Perry's Variety' then it is worth a place in the garden.'

ALICE ARTINDALE
1872–1956

Delphinium 'Alice Artindale'

Some flowers seem to gather to themselves a special aura of romance and desirability. Hundreds of new delphinium varieties are bred and discarded every year, and yet *Delphinium* 'Alice Artindale', now over fifty years old, is still proudly pointed out to visitors by any keen gardener who has managed to acquire it.

This spectacular delphinium was bred by the Sheffield firm of William Artindale and Son, which was founded in the mid-nineteenth century. William's son John had a good head for business, expanding to a six acre nursery at Nether Green, and another at Boston in Lincolnshire. The nurseries grew herbaceous plants, and sold seeds, plants and cut flowers through their own shops and market stalls in Sheffield, as well as issuing a catalogue which ran to over 200 pages.

Delphiniums were a speciality, and although there was no deliberate breeding programme, manager Ted Barker and John Artindale would each year select seedlings which seemed promising. Around 1935 Ted Barker pointed out a young plant which was unusual. Cuttings were taken and it was soon apparent that they had raised a winner. John named it after his wife Alice.

Delphinium 'Alice Artindale' has a strong spike of evenly spaced, azure blue and mauve double flowers. The extra row of petals in each rosette take the place of reproductive organs so that the sterile flowers last longer. This makes it an excellent cut flower, and orders flooded in from customers who saw the new delphinium at Chelsea and other shows.

William Artindale and Son are no longer in horticulture, and delphinium enthusiasts have moved on, setting new rules for what constitutes a prize bloom. Nevertheless *Delphinium* 'Alice Artindale' retains her place in the affections of many gardeners and is still one of the most famous delphiniums ever bred.

A. T. JOHNSON
1873–1956

Ceanothus 'A. T. Johnson'
Cytisus 'Johnson's Crimson'
Erica × *darleyensis* 'Arthur Johnson'
Geranium endressii 'A. T. Johnson'
Geranium 'Johnson's Blue'
Mimulus guttatus 'A. T. Johnson'

Arthur Tysilio Johnson, Welsh schoolmaster, photographer and writer, was a thoughtful, and highly individualistic gardener. With his wife Norah (referred to in his books and articles as The Lady of the Garden), he gardened for fifty years at Tyn-y-Groes in the lower Conway Valley. During that time he subdued and managed what eventually became more than two acres of very varied garden, beside a tumbling mill stream.

Johnson deplored gardeners in a hurry. 'Gardening is not only an art, but a gentle art', he declared, 'you cannot batter into being a garden'. His own garden developed from nothing in clearly defined stages over the five decades, as land was added, a fact which contributed to the pleasure it gave.

The Lady of the Garden was particularly keen on rhododendrons and alpines, while A. T. Johnson became a great shrub enthusiast, and old roses were included in this category. Although their garden began with conventional herbaceous borders, even before the First World War these were transformed into mixed borders with shrubs predominating, hardy plants such as hemerocallis, tradescantia and violas being naturalised in between.

Johnson liked natural gardening, choosing plants to suit the conditions rather than trying to make the conditions suit the plants. Indeed the secret of making and managing his extensive garden without help was that Johnson believed in taking Nature into partnership instead of fighting against her. When conquering new areas he advocated using colonising plants instead of spade and weedkiller. 'We have a friendly regard for plants which not only naturalise, but take entire care of themselves', he wrote, and in those days such emphasis on groundcover plants was a novel way of gardening.

Not surprisingly he valued hardy geraniums. Visiting Glenluce in Scotland a few years before the war, he found on the shores of the bay a variety of the native *Geranium sanguineum* which had large, soft pink flowers. It differed from the more usual Lancastriense form in having no crimson veins, and under the name of 'Glenluce' it is still available.

From his own garden Johnson also selected two outstanding forms of *Geranium endressii* which were put on the market by Ingwersens Nursery. *G. endressii* 'Rose Clair' was salmon pink, while the one that bears his name, *G. endressii* 'A. T. Johnson', was a dwarfer form of soft, silvery pink. Possibly this is no longer in cultivation, for the plant usually sold under this name is more of a flesh pink.

The famous hybrid *Geranium* 'Johnson's Blue' came about by chance around 1945, although helped by the discerning eye of its namesake. He had selected a strain of *Geranium grandiflorum* (now *G. himalayense*), which had especially good colour and size of flower. This crossed with *Geranium pratense*, which was naturalised in the Mill Garden. The resulting hybrid, Johnson reported, 'has proved an excellent border plant'. Sterile, but a vigorous grower, it bore a profusion of large, long-lasting flowers in early summer, of a purer blue, as Johnson observed, than any other geranium he had grown, with the exception of *G. wallichianum* 'Buxton's Variety'.

E. C. Buxton (*qv*) who in the early years lived not far away, was one of many gardening friends, including Graham Thomas, a regular visitor. ATJ, as Johnson often signed himself, had a great knowledge of plants and was happy to share it. In 1931 he wrote a book explaining Latin names, which is still indispensable. He was over the years gardening correspondent of The Times, and The Sunday Times, and in numerous articles and five gardening books he wrote with enthusiasm, humour and expertise about his garden and plants.

One book was on the subject of hardy heathers, of which he was a great advocate. 'You will have some difficulty in naming a shrub more worthy of the gardener's respect', he declared, extolling the long-flowering, weed-smothering habits of *Erica carnea*.

Erica × *darleyensis* 'Arthur Johnson' is a winter-flowering heather of his own raising, a chance cross between, he believed, *E. carnea* 'Ruby Glow' and *E. erigena* 'Hibernica'. He showed the new hybrid at The Royal Horticultural Society in 1952, gaining an

axifraga 'Wada's Variety'

Rosmarinus officinalis 'Severn Sea'

Dicentra 'Boothman's Variety'

Dahlia 'Bishop of Llandaff'

Magnolia × *highdownensis*

Cistus 'Peggy Sammons' (centre) in the author's garden

Delphinium 'Alice Artindale'

Tropaeolum tuberosum 'Ken Aslet'

Lonicera nitida 'Baggesen's Gold', at Kiftsgate Court

Papaver orientale 'Perry's White'

Aquilegia vulgaris 'Nora Barlow'

Viola 'Molly Sanderson'

Award of Merit. Tolerant of lime, and with magenta flowers in sprays nearly ten inches long, it is still one of the best and most widely-grown winter-flowering heathers.

Arthur Johnson was a keen fisherman, and he may well have been out fishing when he found an unusual form of the musk flower, *Mimulus guttatus*, growing beside a stream. The petals were so heavily blotched with red that the normal yellow background was overpowered. He brought some home and grew it along the edge of his own mill stream, where he described it as 'a very charming thing massed along the water, when the stately *Iris sibirica* is belting the banks with blue'.

Another red flower associated with him is a seedling broom which appeared in the garden. In habit like the dainty, white Spanish broom, it covered itself with masses of tiny, all-red flowers. Graham Thomas helped to put it on the market, and *Cytisis* 'Johnson's Crimson' is still among the showiest of the hybrid brooms.

It is to Arthur Johnson that we owe that fine garden plant, *Daphne cneorum* 'Eximia', a form which has flowers as well as leaves well over one third larger than the ordinary *Daphne cneorum* at its best. Johnson was pleased with it, naturally, but modestly named it 'Eximia', meaning 'distinguished', so that its link with him is not widely known.

Only one of the six plants named after A. T. Johnson did not come from his own garden, and that was a hybrid ceanothus which was bred in the 1930's by nurserymen Burkwood and Skipwith. Hardy, with large flower panicles of a deep and pure blue, it has two flowering seasons, one about midsummer and the other in the autumn.

Plants named after Arthur Johnson commemorate a modest and talented man whose beautiful garden was not only inspiring, but gave to future gardeners some outstandingly good plants. He also deserves acknowledgement as a pioneer in the concept of labour-saving gardening, using shrubs with groundcover plants naturalised in between. 'We have all along adopted the strategic measure of at least holding the wild at bay with its own weapons', he declared.

Johnson did not go so far as to claim that gardening by this method was care-free. 'Never an autumn passes', he recorded ruefully just a few years before his death, 'without, on my taking away the garden seats, the Lady of the Garden reminds me that they have never been sat on'.

MAGGIE MOTT

Viola 'Maggie Mott'

Maggie Mott the person remains a tantalising shadow, and the true viola itself is almost as elusive. Many plants now labelled 'Maggie Mott' are somewhat questionable.

Maggie Mott was one of the daughters of Mr Albert Mott and his wife Emma, and at the turn of the century the family lived at a house named Scotswood in Sunningdale, Berkshire. Their gardener was a Mr F. Burdett, who may have been interested in violas enough to breed them, or perhaps he just found a chance seedling. Certainly he must have recognised a plant with outstanding qualities, for in 1902 he arranged for a bluey-mauve viola, named after his employer's daughter, to be exhibited at the Royal Horticultural Society's June Show.

Disappointingly it won no award, but plants of it were donated to the Society's Chiswick garden, and in 1904 a trial of 126 different violas was conducted there. This time 'Maggie Mott' impressed the judges with her flowers of soft, unusually bluey mauve, lightening towards the centre; her vigorous, spreading growth, and exceptionally free-flowering habit.

Dobbies of Edinburgh, a nursery with special interest in violas, lost no time in adding it to their extensive list. Tufted violas were fashionable at the time—William Robinson (*qv*) grew them in quantity at Gravetye, and extolled their virtues in various publications. By 1927 the Royal Horticultural Society Journal was able to record, ' "Maggie Mott" has become everybody's favourite.' She had a rival though, for a viola named 'John Quarton' was almost identical, although more compact in habit, and the two were often confused.

In the 1930's 'Maggie Mott' even flowered proudly in India, when the garden designer John Codrington took a hand in improving the Residency gardens for the Commander in Chief, Sir Philip Chetwode. His wife had set her heart on a large, round pond at the end of a vista, but it was considered too expensive. Instead John Codrington had a sunken, circular bed constructed, with a concrete edge, and planted it entirely with *Viola* 'Maggie Mott'. From the Residency windows it looked for all the world like a stretch of water reflecting the blue Indian sky.

One of the things commending *Viola* 'Maggie Mott', was its vigour, but named varieties often weaken over the years, and this seems to have been no exception. Similar violas are also readily produced from seed, so that it is difficult now to distinguish the true strain.

Of Maggie Mott herself very little can be gleaned. One of her brothers, Major General Stanley Fielder Mott, had a distinguished Army career, and retired to live at Leamington Hastings, near Rugby. In 1948 Maggie Mott was reported to be living there too, but if so she has left no trace. Perhaps she preferred anonymity.

Viola 'Maggie Mott'

MRS POPPLE

Fuchsia 'Mrs Popple'

A t Stevenage between the wars, and next door to the Six Hills Nursery run by Clarence Elliott (*qv*), there lived a Mr and Mrs Popple. They had a tennis court in the garden, at the end of which ran a path and a grass bank, and growing all along the top of the bank were bushes of a vigorous and attractive fuchsia.

A number of small-flowered fuchsias bred from *F. magellanica* were known to be hardy, but this handsome variety had quite large, purple and scarlet flowers. Clarence Elliott noted it when on neighbourly visits, but tender shrubs were not his line of business, and he naturally assumed that cuttings of the bushes would have to be taken every autumn, overwintered in the greenhouse and planted out the following spring. However while visiting one day he was startled to learn that the owners did no such thing. The fuchsia had grown there for a good twenty years it seemed, since before the Popple's time anyway. It was totally hardy.

Clarence Elliott lost no time in begging some cuttings, and in 1934 he exhibited this find at a Royal Horticultural Society Show, under the name *Fuchsia* 'Mrs Popple'. It won an Award of Merit and was an immediate success with the public, as it has been ever since.

Eventually the Popple's garden was bought and built over, disappearing beneath Stevenage New Town. The original source of the bushy, free-flowering fuchsia which grew there remains a mystery.

ROWALLANE AND HUGH ARMYTAGE-MOORE
?–1955

Chaenomeles × *superba* 'Rowallane Hybrid'
Hypericum 'Rowallane'
Primula 'Rowallane Rose'
Viburnum plicatum 'Rowallane'

'The name Rowallane is a hall mark for any plant', Frank Knight, the Director of Wisley Garden, declared in 1950. Indeed Rowallane is a garden that is better known through the plants which bear its name, than for itself.

Situated some twelve miles south of Belfast, in Northern Ireland, the small country estate of Rowallane was bought by the Reverend John Moore in the 1860's. It was a small farm on a barren hillside, but he built sheltering walls to form two kitchen gardens, and planted flowering shrubs, and trees—some seven thousand of them.

In 1903 the place was left to a nephew, Hugh Armytage-Moore, who was working twenty miles away at Castlewellan, as a land agent. The new owner began to design and plant a garden on a grand scale. Trees were thinned, opening up distant views, and the small wall-bound fields were adapted to form a series of gardens within a garden. An extensive Rock Garden was made around a large outcrop of whinstone rock, and damp-loving subjects were planted beside a stream in another of the enclosures. Against the tall walls he planted things thought to need shelter, and paths and cross-paths were planned so as to show both the garden and views of the hills. Gradually more and more farmland was taken in.

A gardening friend reckoned that few men had as good an eye for a plant as Hugh Armytage-Moore, who declared, 'Quality, distinctiveness, individuality, can stand out conspicuously in the plant as in the personage. Good plants form the indispensable material with which to build a good garden'. Accordingly, Moore was discriminating in what he chose. Rhododendrons and azaleas liked the conditions, and he planted great banks of them, some of his own breeding. He was willing to experiment, and many of the new and exciting garden plants then being sent home from the Far East found homes at Rowallane.

In the Walled Garden there was a Celtic cross design in the paving, and in the middle Moore planted a *Viburnum plicatum*, which had been grown from seed brought from China by Ernest Wilson in 1905. Late-flowering, it was less vigorous than some other forms, but had a neat habit and its flat, white flower heads turned to a crop of showy fruits in the autumn. Friends were given cuttings and young plants, and it became known as *Viburnum plicatum* 'Rowallane'. In 1942 Captain Collingwood Ingram (*qv*) exhibited the shrub at the Royal Horticultural Society where it gained an Award of Merit.

Hugh Armytage-Moore was a quiet, modest man, and only occasionally exhibited plants himself. About 1920 a seedling was noticed at Rowallane which was thought to be a cross between *Chaenomeles speciosa*, and the smaller *C. japonica*. It was left to grow on, and proved to have large, blood-red flowers on a low-growing bush. Moore showed it at the RHS in 1950, but at that time it did not find favour with the judges. Since then *Chaenomeles × superba* 'Rowallane' has been recognised as one of the best of the red-flowered varieties, succeeding in sun or half shade, in any average soil.

Shrubs were probably Hugh Armytage-Moore's greatest love, but he also collected at Rowallane a vast range of choice alpine, herbaceous and bog plants. Beside the stream grew candelabra primulas, and one of them came to be known as 'Rowallane Rose'. A strong-growing, pink-flowered hybrid, with *Primula pulverulenta* likely as one of its parents, this relies on vegetative propagation, since it sets no seed.

Rowallane was blessed with the devoted services of William Watson who, as Head Gardener, worked in partnership with Armytage-Moore for twenty-four years. Also Slieve Donard was nearby, one of Ireland's greatest nurseries, and proprietor Leslie Slinger, besides being a supplier, became a friend and frequent visitor. It was he who, in 1932, pointed out a self-sown seedling hypericum in the Rock Garden. This was halfway between two slightly tender Himalayan species, *Hypericum leschenaulti* and *H. hookeranum* 'Rogersii', and their progeny was soon recognised as a real treasure.

Hypericum 'Rowallane' grows some 6ft (1.8m) tall, and in late summer great yellow bowl-shaped flowers are borne in clusters on the young arching branches. Hard winters may cut it right back to the roots, usually without harm, although it is not suitable for really cold gardens. With blooms larger than *Hypericum* 'Hidcote', and a long flowering season, this shrub has been described as 'Queen of the St John's Worts, the finest of all hypericums'. Slieve Donard Nursery put the plant into commerce, and it has become a famous and much-loved shrub.

Hugh Armytage-Moore died in 1955, and Rowallane was taken over by the National Trust. Being in Northern Ireland the garden is not as much visited as it deserves, but its named plants are very well regarded. This would have pleased Hugh Armytage-Moore, who once remarked, 'I would rather be remembered as a plant selector, than a plant collector'.

Chaenomeles x superba 'Rowallane Hybrid'

THE WARHAM SNOWDROP

Galanthus plicatus 'Warham Variety'

The Warham Snowdrop is a legacy of the Crimean War. As a symbol of that tragic war the snowdrop is apt, for the British army taking part in the 1854 siege of Sebastopol had to withstand the horrors of a Russian winter. When Spring finally came those soldiers who survived were heartened by the sight of snowdrops pushing up through the melting snow.

The Crimean snowdrop, *Galanthus plicatus*, is larger than our native snowdrop, with curled back leaves, but it reminded the cold and war-weary soldiers of home. One officer by the name of Captain Adlington dug up a clump and sent it back to his Norfolk home near Swaffham.

The bulbs thrived, and in due course Mrs Adlington gave some to a friend who lived at Warham in Norfolk. She in turn gave bulbs away to her cowherd's wife, a Mrs Buttle, in whose garden they became quite a colony. The Reverend Charles T. Digby, Rector of Warham, happened to be something of a snowdrop enthusiast, and in 1916 he sent blooms of it to E. A. Bowles (*qv*), a great authority on the genus. Mrs Buttle was soon receiving requests for her snowdrop bulbs from Bowles and other snowdrop fanciers, and it became known as the Warham Snowdrop.

Clumps of the Crimean snowdrop were also brought home by other soldiers, but the Warham form was, in the opinion of experts, larger and finer than the type. *Galanthus plicatus* is however notoriously promiscuous. Not only does it interbreed with other species, but the bulbs tend to lose vigour as they age, and numerous seedlings spring up to replace the old bulbs. The Warham Snowdrop is still commercially listed, but some experts doubt whether, more than seventy years after its discovery in a Norfolk cowman's garden, the real Warham Snowdrop still exists.

BENENDEN AND 'CHERRY' INGRAM
1880–1981

Rosmarinus officinalis 'Benenden Blue'
Primula 'Ingram's Blue'
Rubus × *tridel* 'Benenden'

At the end of the First World War Captain Collingwood Ingram left the Royal Flying Corps and with his wife bought a house in the Kentish village of Benenden. A scholarly, energetic man with a scientific mind, Ingram was first interested in birds, but he wanted to make useful scientific discoveries and felt that ornithology no longer offered such potential. Final disillusionment came when he read an earnest article on the number of times a Great Tit defecated every 24 hours. 'I concluded it was high time I occupied my thoughts with some other aspect of nature', he recorded drily. 'I chose plants.'

There was land but no garden to speak of around The Grange. Ingram planted a shelter belt of trees, studied botany from books and then travelled abroad on the first of many plant hunting trips. Over the next half century he created a series of sylvan glades planted mainly with trees, shrubs and plants which he brought home as seedlings from places as far apart as Japan and Patagonia, Portugal and New Zealand. Each plant and tree became a memento of some visit, and when in 1970 he wrote a book about his plants and planting he called it 'A Garden of Memories'.

Ingram first became well-known in the twenties as a world authority on cherries, leading to his nickname of 'Cherry' Ingram. Among the species and varieties accumulated from Japan and elsewhere at least fifty had never been seen in England before. He also produced many new hybrid varieties.

Hybridising plants was an absorbing hobby from the start, satisfying both his scientific and gardening interests. 'The creation of a really first-class plant', he asserted, 'will give you not only a temporary thrill but a lasting glow of satisfaction'.

The delightful hybrid rubus that he bred has certainly given pleasure to many gardeners. Its creation stemmed from a visit to

Mexico in 1938 by plant hunters E. K. Balls and W. Balfour Gourlay. They brought back seed of *Rubus trilobus*, a member of the bramble family, which they found growing on an extinct volcano. Subsequently Ingram was given two rooted cuttings.

When these flowered, their pure white blooms were large but not numerous, so he tried crossing the species with a more floriferous relative, *Rubus deliciosus*. The result was a triumph. The hybrid offspring had thornless arching boughs some 8ft (2.5m) high, which in early summer were smothered with pure white flowers 2in (6cm) across, each one tufted with golden stamens.

Collingwood Ingram exhibited the new hybrid at the Royal Horticultural Society in 1947. Combining the names of the two parents, he called it *Rubus × tridel*, adding 'Benenden' to indicate its origin. It has since received every award the RHS can bestow on a plant, and its enduring popularity makes it Ingram's most successful creation.

The rubus was not however one of his own favourites. He was very keen on rhododendrons, and produced numerous hybrids, many of which he named after birds. He also hybridised gladiolus and cistus. Most of the former have not endured, but *Cistus* 'Anne Palmer', which he named after the owner of Rosemoor in Devon, remains an easy and popular shrub. He liked and bred primroses, and *Primula* 'Tomato Red', and *P.* 'Ingram's Blue' which has dark foliage, are still commercially available. The only other plant actually named after the village of Benenden was a rosemary. *Rosmarinus officinalis* 'Benenden Blue' did not come about through experimentation, but was discovered about 1930 on a Mediterranean trip, as a result of a car accident.

Rounding a bend too fast near Sartène in Corsica, the driver of Ingram's hired car scraped a vehicle coming the other way, and the two drivers immediately set to in voluble argument. Shrewdly estimating that this ritual would take some time, Ingram wandered off to look for plants. What he found was a rosemary with narrow, feathery leaves, softer and infinitely more aromatic than usual, and whereas the common rosemary has rather washed-out blue flowers, this shrub had blooms of a striking sapphire blue. A seedling was successfully dug up, brought home and grown at Benenden, where it proved able to survive most English winters if grown in a very dry spot with full sun.

Collingwood Ingram regularly opened his garden to the public, and was active, energetic and astringent right up to his death at the age of one hundred. Towards the end, many of his special plants were entrusted to a great friend and rhododendron enthusiast, Alan Hardy. Just before he died Ingram asked his friend to take home seedlings of a particularly treasured hybrid rhododendron, *R.* × *ludorum*. Hardy went to assure Ingram that the seedlings had been dug up safely, and the old man put out a thin hand. 'If I get better', he said with spirit, 'I want them back!'

Rubus x tridel 'Benenden'

SIX HILLS NURSERY AND CLARENCE ELLIOTT
1881–1969

Nepeta mussinii 'Six Hills Giant'
Penstemon 'Six Hills Hybrid'
Saxifraga umbrosa primuloides 'Elliott's Variety'

Six Hills Nursery on the Great North Road at Stevenage was founded by Clarence Elliott in 1907, when he was twenty-six. He had trained with Backhouse of York (*qv*), a large nursery famous for its alpines, and then spent several years fruit growing in Africa. Alpines were however his great love, and Six Hills was one of the few nurseries then specialising in these plants.

Clarence Elliott became one of the best known and most respected personalities in the gardening world, and was a founder member of the Alpine Garden Society. He was an outstanding cultivator of these exacting plants, many of which he collected whilst on expeditions to The Alps, Corsica, Chile and the Falkland Islands.

Old cottage plants were another of Elliott's interests and he urged people to make room in their gardens for antique plants as well as new species and modern varieties. Asking for bits of interesting plants from gardens he visited, or merely passed, was part of the fun, and he cherished the idea of a leisurely plant collecting trip touring villages in England and Scotland. The ideal car for this he reckoned would be 'incapable of exceeding twenty-miles per hour and would come equipped with seed envelopes and a fishing rod'. Whether the fishing rod was for use near water or for reaching over fences for bits of plants to strike as cuttings was left unclear.

A piece begged from a local garden gave Clarence Elliott the nursery's most famous plant. The Russian catmint, *Nepeta mussinii*, had been cultivated in England for over a century. About 1934 Elliott noticed in a local garden a form which was much taller than normal with larger flowers, and he was given an offshoot. The ease with which catmint can be propagated must make it a nurseryman's dream, and this one plant was soon worked up to a saleable stock and named *Nepeta mussinii* 'Six Hills Giant'. It was so popular that the original form is now seldom grown.

In those days growing alpines was a relatively new idea and the market was not large. Having four acres of land, Six Hills therefore grew a number of herbaceous plants which helped to support the alpine side. New varieties of herbaceous plants were called after the nursery, notably a strain of *Linum narbonense*, and strongly scented lupins but, along with *Viola* 'Elliott's White', they are probably no longer grown. However a chance seedling from *Penstemon roezlii* resulted in a hardy hybrid which has endured. Named *Penstemon* 'Six Hills Hybrid', it grows only 7in (21cm) high but up to 18in (45cm) across when happy, and has masses of rosy-lilac flowers.

A few years before the First World War Clarence Elliott went on a trip to the Alps. There he spotted a plant of *Saxifraga umbrosa primuloides*, a near relation of the familiar London Pride, but this particular plant, besides being dwarf, had unusually deep pink flowers. When stocks were sufficient to sell, Six Hills exhibited the new plant at one of the Royal Horticultural Society Shows as *Saxifraga umbrosa primuloides* 'Elliott's Variety'. Unfortunately Elliott's friend Walter Ingwersen had a neighbouring stand on which stood one exactly similar labelled *S. umbrosa primuloides* 'Ingwersen's Variety'. He also collected plants in the Alps. No-one could discover any difference between them, and to this day the plants are still sold under separate names.

Six Hills Nursery was a large concern, and Elliott had as a financial partner one Commander Clive Pinsent, whose wife is commemorated in *Saxifraga* 'Kathleen Pinsent', while his sister-in-law Molly Pinsent appears as a *Campanula carpatica*.

Clarence Elliott was witty as well as erudite and much in demand for newspaper and magazine articles, through which he helped to popularise the growing of alpine plants. In 1946 he retired to concentrate on writing, and went to live near his son Joe (*qv*) who ran an alpine nursery in Gloucestershire. Six Hills Nursery carried on for a while under his erstwhile manager and friend Frank Barker, but the nursery closed when he died, not long after. Although referred to as 'the late Mr Clarence Elliott' in the Royal Horticultural Society's Journal of 1962, Elliott continued to grow alpines and write about them until his death in 1969.

It is perhaps incongruous that the best known Six Hills variety grown today should be a large, acquisitive herbaceous plant, the very antithesis of the dainty alpines Clarence Elliott loved. He was however a great plantsman and there is no doubt that the catmint he made famous is a very good plant indeed.

Clarence Elliott

MARY HENRY
1884–?

Phlox 'Chattahoochee'

Not many mountains seem to be named after women, but in Western Canada there is a peak called Mount Mary Henry. It commemorates an energetic, enthusiastic gardener and botanist who, in the 1930's and 40's when her five children had grown up, began to explore North America looking for plants. It was said that she discovered more new plants in the United States than anyone else, and she made over fifty expeditions. Engineers planned part of the Alaskan Highway using her information on one unmapped area.

Mrs J. Norman Henry gardened in Philadelphia, and dwarf phlox were one of her specialities because, she said, they were so beautiful and useful in the rock garden. She was able to put over twenty-five new varieties into cultivation, including *Phlox stolonifera* 'Blue Ridge', and *Phlox* 'Chattahoochee'.

It was on an expedition to the Southern States that Mary Henry came across the latter, growing near the Chattahoochee River which forms part of the border between Alabama and Georgia. About 8in (20cm) high, the plant is possibly a naturally occurring hybrid between *Phlox divaricata* and *P. pilosa*. Its silky, lavender blue flowers have a brilliant crimson centre, and in cool, moist soils it spreads into a lax cushion of harmonious colour. Mary Henry's enthusiastic description is apt: 'It is a most spectacular plant'.

When exploring rough and remote country, she had to cope with rattlesnakes (a small and specially sharpened spade decapitated them), thorns, bogs, creeks, insects and on one occasion three armed men with hostile intentions. She shrugged off such hazards cheerfully, as part of the adventure, and went on collecting plants.

Many were taken back to her own garden, Gladwyne, where they had to cope with Philadelphia's winters. She grew over fifty different trilliums, a stunning range of lilies, azaleas, penstemons, and other American natives, most of which she had collected herself. 'Although the plants from a warmer clime have a rough time', she reported, 'success in acclimatising them has been great and I have been able to bring into cultivation some hundreds of new plants.'

A modest and unassuming woman, it is a pity that Mary Henry is not well known to modern gardeners, who have benefited from the lovely plants she collected.

Phlox `Chatterhoochee`

NORAH LEIGH
1884–1970

Phlox paniculata 'Norah Leigh'
Viola 'Norah Leigh'

The variegated *Phlox* 'Norah Leigh' is a plant for the connoisseur. Its leaves are richly marked with cream and a large clump makes a real border highlight, yet its exact origin is unknown. *Phlox paniculata* 'Variegata' with similar pinky-lilac flowers, was grown for many years in Munich's Botanic Garden, but there is no evidence that the two are connected.

Norah Leigh was the mother-in-law of alpine nurseryman Joe Elliott (*qv*), and a keen gardener. For years she grew this striking phlox in the garden at Broadwell Manor in the Cotswolds, but although it had originally been given to her she could not remember by whom. She passed cuttings to her son-in-law who named it after her and propagated it. In due course a plant was also given to Alan Bloom of Bressingham Nursery, but he found that it was susceptible to eelworm and slow to propagate, since new plants grown from root cuttings do not carry the variegation.

As a result of this difficulty in reproducing the plant in quantity, *Phlox paniculata* 'Norah Leigh' has remained scarce and sought after. It is not the easiest plant to keep happy either, and although it must have originated elsewhere, today's gardeners have Norah Leigh to thank for cherishing it in her garden all those years.

She also grew a viola which originated as a chance seedling in the garden. Probably one parent was *V. cornuta* but this plant proved to be much more compact, with neat pads of leaves and a continuous succession of rounded, soft lavender blooms from spring until late autumn. Such a useful plant deserved to be passed on, and, naming it *Viola* 'Norah Leigh' Joe Elliott included it in his stock. His nursery is now closed but this pleasing little viola is still available.

HIGHDOWN AND COL SIR FREDERICK STERN
1884–1967

Clematis × *vedrariensis* 'Highdown'
Magnolia × *highdownensis*
Rose 'Highdownensis'
Rose 'Wedding Day'

Frederick Claude Stern became something of a horticultural pioneer in the early 1900's. He had been born into a merchant banking family, and as a young man at the turn of the century, enjoyed amateur steeplechasing and big game hunting in Africa, but by 1909 he had bought himself a house in Sussex. Aptly named 'Highdown', it perched on the South Downs, facing the sea near Worthing.

Its land encompassed a large, old chalk pit, which had been used for keeping pigs and hens. The garden around the house consisted of little more than two sloping lawns, and, wishing to play tennis, Stern realised that the only place flat enough for a court was the base of the chalk pit. The tennis court was duly made, but the surroundings of ramshackle pigsties and chicken refuse was hardly conducive to smart tennis parties, so he decided to clear them away and try planting shrubs and other plants.

No-one could advise on what should be planted, and several people suggested he give up the idea of trying to grow anything on virgin chalk. Three knowledgeable friends encouraged him, however, suggesting that he should mulch with chicken manure and leafmould, and then experiment on an area of chalk scree, where part of the 30ft (10m) high cliff had slipped.

Stern studied geological maps, and decided that plants which came from the Mediterranean would probably be tolerant of lime. Experimenting with these and others, he gradually realised that many plants, shrubs and trees would not only grow in such unpromising conditions, but do well. The secret was to choose lime-tolerant plants, to break up the chalk, enabling their roots to penetrate, and to plant things when they were young.

In 1912 the famous nursery of James Veitch held a closing down sale, and Frederick Stern attended, buying many plants which had been sent back from China by the plant explorer, E. H. Wilson. A surprising number subsequently flourished in the chalk pit, where by now the cultivated area was quite extensive. The success of these Chinese plants led him to subscribe to other Far Eastern collecting expeditions; a friend living in Greece sent him Mediterranean seeds, bulbs and corms; and knowledgeable gardeners began to visit and exchange plants.

Service in the First World War interrupted Stern's garden making. Afterwards he served briefly as Private Secretary to Lloyd George, considering a political career, but the idea was eventually discarded. He became particularly interested in the scientific aspects of gardening, examining sections of plants under a microscope to ascertain their chromosome numbers, with a view to hybridisation. 'It is an exciting amusement to cross plants and raise new forms, and after some time to see the results', he declared enthusiastically. This hobby soon required the digging up of the paddock and purchase of extra land in order to grow more plants.

Stern found that eremurus, the Foxtail Lilies, grew well on chalk, and he produced a range of hybrids known as *Eremurus* 'Highdown Hybrids'—now no longer a distinct strain. He tried his hand at breeding a number of other genera, including lilies, irises, hellebores and tree peonies. He also experimented with daffodils, producing cultivars 'Goring', 'Kingston', 'Amberley' and 'Handcross', all named after local villages. In this activity he was given helpful advice by P. D. Williams of Lanarth (*qv*), and so became acquainted with his cousin J. C. Williams, of Caerhayes in Cornwall. J. C. Williams' passion was camellias, but he had also planted a great many magnolias at Caerhayes, and in 1927 he sent Frederick Stern three seedling magnolias just a few inches high, unnamed because the label had been mislaid.

Generally magnolias dislike very limey conditions, but these were duly planted, and somewhat to Stern's surprise all three flourished and grew into bushy trees, about 15ft (4.5m) high. Their mass of hanging, white flowers with maroon centres won an Award of Merit when Stern exhibited branches at the Royal Horticultural Society in 1937.

A botanist decided that the trees were hybrids of *Magnolia sinensis* and *M. wilsonii*, and named the new plant *Magnolia × highdownensis*. Stern was not entirely convinced, especially as the seeds bred absolutely true, and some botanists now regard

Highdown's magnolia as a particularly good form of *Magnolia wilsonii*. The original trees were lost in the great storm of 1987, but seed had been saved, and young plants have now been grown to replace them.

Stern tried repeatedly to grow the large-flowered garden varieties of clematis, but they evidently disliked the chalk. 'An unhappy plant is an eyesore in any garden', he said briskly, and instead resorted to small-flowered and specie clematis. On the east side of the house he planted *Clematis × vedrariensis*, a small-flowered hybrid with *C. montana* as one of its parents. 'The flowers are a good pink, and it is the strongest grower of any clematis tried here', he recorded. 'In fact it has to be cut back periodically, otherwise it covers all the windows and becomes a nuisance'. His plant had particularly attractive, bronzy foliage, and is now commercially available as *Clematis × vedrariensis* 'Highdown'.

Highdown was not created and maintained single-handedly. Sybil Stern, whom Frederick had married in 1919, was whole-heartedly involved in the garden, and her husband always acknowledged that he owed a great deal to the help of his old gardener, Mr Buckman.

The garden in the chalk pit developed over the years, and eventually included rock gardens and two ponds, interspersed with pleasing walks broadening into lawns and narrowing again between mixed groups of trees and shrubs. These were widely underplanted with bulbs. A visitor in spring would not easily banish from mind the sheets of snowdrops, and carpets of blue anemones, which had shown their liking for the conditions by multiplying gloriously. It was not, however, a garden that was easy to look after. For one thing Stern liked plants to seed themselves, so that he only allowed hoeing in the vegetable garden and nursery area. Everywhere else was hand-weeded.

Rose 'Highdownensis', a particularly good form of *Rosa moyesii*, was one reward of this policy. The original *R. moyesii* plants sold by James Veitch were grown from Chinese seed, and had vivid red, single flowers, followed by huge flagon-shaped heps. About 1924 the specimen planted at Highdown produced a seedling, which was noticed and grown on. Although not quite such a good colour as the original, this proved to have more flowers to the cluster, to be bushier in habit, and as an added bonus the young shoots had coppery leaves and colourful prickles. Except for the flower colour, it was a better plant than its parent in every way, prompting the rose expert, Graham Thomas, to remark that at both flowering and fruiting time it could hold its own with anything in the garden.

The Sterns experimented with many roses, finding that most tolerated the extremely limey conditions. One of Highdown's more unusual roses was *Rosa sino-wilsonii*, a strong bush with bronze leaves and stems. It was, however, rather shy about producing its clusters of white, single flowers, and so, seeking a hardier plant with pink flowers and bronze foliage, Stern crossed it with *Rosa moyesii*.

Some of the resulting seedlings showed a tendency to climb, but had only sparse pink-flowers. 'One has to be ruthless when hybridising, to throw out and destroy all hybrids which are not up to the highest standard', Sir Frederick Stern declared firmly, and the ungardenworthy seedlings were duly jettisoned.

Others from the cross, however, had bronzy stems and made big bushy plants, covered with apricot buds which opened to white, single flowers. Seed from the best of these plants was sown, and one of the resultant offspring was a vigorous climber. Sweetly-scented flower clusters made a mass over the whole plant, the yellow buds changing to pure-white flowers. The flowers opened for the first time on the 26th of June, which happened to be the Stern's wedding anniversary. 'There are many disappointments in breeding', remarked Stern, 'but sometimes one gets a winner which is a thrill, making up for all the waiting'. This distinctive rose, which was soon completely covering a cherry tree, was patently a winner. Romantically named 'Wedding Day', it was exhibited at the RHS in 1950, and has increased in popularity ever since.

Frederick Stern wrote scholarly treatises on peonies, and on snowdrops and snowflakes, genera which particularly interested him. He helped to rescue the ailing Botanical Magazine, was Chairman of the John Innes Horticultural Institution, and played an active role in the Royal Horticultural Society, of which he became a Vice President. In 1956 he received a knighthood for 'services to horticulture'. Despite his various activities, he also found time to write about the making of Highdown in a book, 'The Chalk Garden', published in 1960, seven years before his death. This enquiring, scientifically-minded gardener had confounded the sceptical by showing that it was possible to make a beautiful garden on chalk, even in the most unpromising conditions.

After her husband's death, Lady Stern generously gave Highdown garden to Worthing Borough Council, and it remains open to the public.

NORA BARLOW
1885–1989

Aquilegia vulgaris 'Nora Barlow'

Nora Darwin was the granddaughter of Charles Darwin, and grew up amidst a troupe of talented aunts, uncles and cousins. She inherited a love of gardening from both sides of the family, but particularly from her mother, who created a garden in Cambridge once described as 'an image of Paradise, where the blackbirds sang all day long in the mossy apple trees, and where every flower was a new discovery'. In later years Nora and her sister gave it to the University for the building of New Hall.

At the age of twenty-six Nora married Alan Barlow, and in the following years brought up six children. She somehow found time to edit several scholarly books about her grandfather and his work, and also to garden enthusiastically.

Just before the war Alan Barlow was knighted, and in 1945 inherited the family baronetcy. By then they were already living at his father's home of Boswells, in Buckinghamshire, whose garden Alan had for many years taken an interest in planning. The soil was decidedly alkaline, and Nora was initially dismayed at the prospect of gardening in such chalky conditions. Through perseverance, however, and helped by advice from Sir Frederick Stern of Highdown (*qv*), she helped to introduce more shrubs, roses and perennials, in place of bedding out plants. The garden had lovely herbaceous borders, largely planned by her husband, sheets of blue anemones in Spring, and unexpected little corners where she grew alpines.

Nora studied genetics at Cambridge, and remained fascinated by the subject. From early on she tried her hand at hybridising various flowers, including aquilegias—her experiments indicated by little muslin bags over the flower heads. On one occasion however she unwisely showed her children how to break off an aquilegia's spur and suck out the honey. Thereafter quite a few of her experiments were tampered with.

The double aquilegia which has become known as 'Nora Barlow' was grown in the garden at Boswells for many years. The flower was pointed out by its namesake as an oddity, but it was almost certainly not bred by her, since a similar form was known as far back as the sixteenth century. With layers of fringed petals in deep rose and white, it is very distinctive, and surprisingly comes true from seed. It was this fact which led to it being commercially marketed. A friend of Nora's suggested to Alan Bloom of Bressingham that he might like to stock this unusual flower, and he was given seed on condition that the aquilegia was named 'Nora Barlow'.

Lady Barlow's own preference was for elegantly simple flowers, whereas the many-petalled *Aquilegia vulgaris* 'Nora Barlow' could be described as fussy. It has proved so popular, however, that the fame of Charles Darwin's gardening granddaughter is assured for many years to come.

Nora Barlow, just before her 100th birthday

PRIMLEY BOTANIC NURSERY AND HERBERT WHITLEY
1886–1955

Hebe 'Primley Gem'
Malva sylvestris 'Primley Blue'
Rosmarinus officinalis 'Primley Blue'

It is no coincidence that all the cultivars bearing the name 'Primley' have blue flowers, for they are the legacy of Herbert Whitley, a shy, clever and eccentric millionaire to whom blue was a very special colour.

The Whitley's family business was the Liverpool brewing firm of Greenall Whitley, and in 1904, following the death of Herbert's father, his mother bought the Primley Estate, at Paignton in Devon. Young Herbert, then studying at Cambridge, had been an enthusiastic breeder of racing pigeons for years, and his elder brother William knew and loved horses, so together they set up in business. The plan was to create a breeding centre for pedigree farm and domestic livestock. Landowners would be able to visit, and stock their estates with the best of everything from turkeys to beef cattle, sporting dogs to shire horses.

The idea was a good one, and the Whitleys had an excellent eye for quality. Soon Primley stock was winning prizes in shows all over the country. After the First World War however, William left to farm, leaving Herbert to run the large estate and breeding stock business. He had a particular penchant for blue, which was evident even in the animals he bred—there were 'Primley Blue' turkeys, 'Blue Silky' poultry, 'Barless Blue' pigeons, even 'Blue Albion' cattle.

Primley House itself had sixteen large greenhouses, and by 1920 Herbert had filled them with tropical and tender plants, a staggering collection that was considered among the best in the country. Plants with blue flowers, foliage or fruit had a special place, naturally, he even had a rare blue water lily. In the greenhouses Whitley would only allow soap and water to be sprayed against pests, to ensure the health of his cherished stick insects which lived and multiplied happily in the tropical jungle. Strangers might also be taken aback to come face to face with young alligators or rare snakes.

Visitors generally came only by invitation, for Herbert Whitley fought shy of people in general—and women in particular, although he had a few trusted women employees. 'The very rustle of a strange skirt and Whitley would have gone to earth', a friend recalled, 'or if caught in his study, disappear in the self-propelled lift in which he would be transported upstairs like some pantomime genie.'

With men who shared his love and knowledge of animals and plants, however, Whitley was warm and generous. It helped too if they were not used to turning in early, for he liked to play snooker and engage in stimulating discussion far into the night. Whitley hardly slept, and once boasted that he had not been to bed for twenty years, merely dossed down on the sofa with a rug over him whenever sleep was necessary.

His collection of exotic animals was increasing, and around 1920 he began planning a full scale private zoo, covering seventy acres. As part of this ambitious project the Primley Botanic Nursery was created, in order to provide hundreds of choice trees and shrubs for the zoo. Herbert Whitley did nothing by halves.

By this time the Primley Estate was the largest employer in Paignton, and Whitley was usually to be seen working harder than most, in an ancient patched jacket, sandals and shabby flannel trousers held up with an old tie. Money meant very little to him, although he insisted on economies such as using secondhand envelopes for estate correspondence; and it was a brave employee who asked for a rise. His swearing was regarded with awe, and it was said that he could spot a slacker as quickly as culling a faulty pigeon.

The zoo was intended to be private, but by 1923 pressure from local townspeople was such that Whitley relented and allowed public access. His was a mind aglow with the scientific wonders of nature, and he saw his zoo as educational. Disgust therefore, at being liable for an Entertainment Tax caused him to close the zoo again for several years.

Paignton Zoo was regarded as one of the finest in Britain, and on Herbert Whitley's death in 1955, aged sixty-nine, a trust was set up which ensured that its educational, scientific and conservationist role continues. Whitley was a very keen conservationist, far ahead of his time, and it is to him that we owe the wildlife sanctuary of Slapton Ley, a unique coastal wetland area south of Dartmouth.

Horrified by a developer's plan to drain it and build a holiday centre, Whitley bought the whole estate in 1921, and often went there to enjoy the richness of its animal, bird and plant life.

It may well have been at Slapton that he found the blue form of the common mallow, which by 1929 was already being sold as *Malva sylvestris* 'Primley Blue'. He would have been delighted with its mass of smoky blue, dark-veined flowers, borne for weeks in the summer. Identical forms have occasionally been found in the wild since then, but it is quite tricky to grow successfully in gardens. It dislikes too rich a soil, is a martyr to rust, and a really hard winter is liable to carry it off. Late summer cuttings take fairly easily however, and this lovely plant is worth any amount of trouble.

The hebe known as 'Primley Gem', has in its time also been called *Hebe* 'Primley Blue', and later *H.* 'Margery Fish'. Its spikes of violet-blue flowers whiten with age, and are borne from July through to late autumn. In winter the leaves of this small shrub turn an attractive bronze; it is relatively hardy, and would have been a useful shrub at the zoo, providing low screening and late colour.

Herbert Whitley had a prodigious memory and never kept records, so that the exact origin of the rosemary offered by Primley Botanic Nursery is unknown. *Rosmarinus officinalis* 'Primley Blue' is semi-prostrate, with a spread of up to 6ft (1.8m), and it bears mid-blue flowers all through a mild winter. Another seedling rosemary from Primley was given to Whitley's friend Norman Hadden (*qv*), and under the name *Rosemarinus officinalis* 'Severn Sea' became one of the best known dark-flowered varieties.

'If, as is said, only a hairline separates genius from eccentricity', a friend remarked after his death, 'then Whitley was the perfect example'. He was shy, intelligent, stimulating and dedicated, as well as being a rough-tongued, argumentative, intolerant misogynist. Whichever side of this remarkable character people encountered, there was no doubt that Herbert Whitley lived life on his terms, and lived it to the full.

CONSTANCE SPRY
1886–1960

Rose 'Constance Spry'
Symphoricarpos albus 'Constance Spry'

The name of Constance Spry is always associated with flower arranging, an art which she revolutionised. Her spectacular arrangements were however backed by an extensive knowledge of plants, many of which she grew in a succession of gardens, and Constance Spry saw herself as a gardener first.

At the age of fourteen she moved with her family to Ireland, and in due course trained there as a Health Lecturer. Later, in London, she became a successful Headmistress of an East End school. It was always brightened with flowers from her garden, and her flair for arranging flowers led to so many commissions from friends that in 1928 she set up her own shop.

In those days decorating with flowers was bound by rigid conventions, inevitably incorporating carnations and asparagus fern, with banks of pot plants for weddings. 'A church should not look like a conservatory'. Constance Spry declared briskly, and instead did large flower arrangements on pedestals, then a novel idea. She hated clichés of style and of material, and urged people to accept no rules. 'Let the flowers remind you of how they looked when growing', she said, and would herself happily use wild clematis from the hedgerows, decorative kale, or leek seed heads in arresting arrangements. She set much store by form and line, with colour in bold patches, and pioneered the use of off-beat colours such as smoky pink and lime green.

Constance Spry was always anxious to learn about and grow new flowers. In 1931 when she was living in Hertfordshire, there was a sale at nearby Aldenham Court, home of a notable gardener and plant collector, the Hon Vicary Gibbs. He had run a nursery, and at the closing-down sale Constance acquired amongst other things some snowberry bushes. When established in her garden they turned out to bear their attractive, white berries in unusually thick clusters, and were much admired. In time the variety was marketed by Sunningdale Nurseries as *Symphoricarpus albus* 'Constance Spry'. She was pleased by the honour, and it is a pity

115

that nowadays the variety is so hard to find.

Graham Thomas of Sunningdale Nurseries was keen on old roses and found in Mrs Spry a fellow enthusiast. At that time these were so out of favour with gardeners and nurserymen that many were in danger of extinction, but Constance Spry collected over fifty, including 'Cardinal de Richelieu', 'Madame Pierre Oger', and 'Variegata de Bologna'. She loved their profusion of wonderfully scented blooms and did not mind that they flowered only briefly. 'What of it?' she said. 'There are other delights to follow, and I would rather have perfection once than a well-maintained level of something else.'

Constance Spry died at the age of seventy, having founded a famous School of Cookery and Home Decoration, and turned flower arranging into a popular art. In 1961, a year after her death, David Austin, then an up-and-coming Wolverhampton nurseryman, launched a new rose. His aim was to bring back to modern roses the scent and many-petalled flowers of the old roses, and this newcomer was the offspring of a Gallica rose, 'Belle Isis', and the Floribunda 'Dainty Maid'. Although Austin had never met Mrs Spry, he wanted to honour those gardeners such as Gertrude Jekyll, Vita Sackville-West and Constance Spry, whose enthusiasm for old roses had inspired and encouraged him, and so he named it 'Constance Spry'.

The rose proved to be a winner. With large pink, cabbagey flowers and strong scent, 'Constance Spry' combines the best characteristics of the old roses with the vigour and strong constitution developed by modern breeders. Although officially a shrub rose, it needs stout support and can be used as a climber. In June the rose bears its enormous, many-petalled flowers in breathtaking profusion, their myrrh-like fragrance heavy on the air. Unfortunately it blooms only once, but Constance Spry, gifted exponent of an essentially ephemeral art, would not have minded that. Flowers may be only a fleeting pleasure, but as she herself once remarked, 'Anticipation and memory endure'.

E. B. ANDERSON
1886–1971

Oxalis 'Beatrix Anderson'
Pulmonaria longifolia 'Bertram Anderson'
Sedum 'Bertram Anderson'
Thymus citriodorus 'Bertram Anderson'

Edward Bertram Anderson used to wonder if there was a gene associated with a love of gardening—if so this outgoing, modest man was a born gardener. By profession however he was a research chemist whose career dictated frequent moves, so that he made and left six gardens in places as diverse as Dublin and Rickmansworth, Devon and Cheshire. Finally he settled for the last ten years of his life at Lower Slaughter in the Cotswolds.

'One can make a garden on anything provided one has patience and is willing to experiment', he once remarked. He himself had both these attributes, plus an intelligent, questioning mind and such a generous nature that he made gardening friends wherever he went.

Anderson was a founder member of the Alpine Garden Society and alpines were his greatest love. He had a full-time job and, as he said, 'This form of gardening requires neither broad acres nor a deep pocket nor abundant leisure, and can give in a small space all the refreshment a hobby should'. He enjoyed plant hunting holidays, and also exchanged plants and seeds with correspondents all over the world, so that he was responsible for introducing a great many plants new to British gardening.

It was an oxalis sent by a Patagonian friend which provided the parent of *Oxalis* 'Beatrix Anderson'. *Oxalis laciniata* is a dwarf plant with large, veined flowers in shades of lilac and pink. In Anderson's Cotswold garden it crossed with *O. enneaphylla*, another South American species. The resultant offspring had pleated-looking leaves like *O. enneaphylla* and somewhat larger flowers than *O. laciniata*. 'I now have several varieties of this hybrid', recorded Anderson, 'and they are distinct and attractive'. The seedlings differed slightly in colour and were given to alpine enthusiast friends. After his death one strain with lilac-coloured flowers was named *Oxalis* 'Ione Hecker', after a gardening friend, and another with pinker flowers, *O.* 'Beatrix Anderson' in remembrance of his violinist wife Trix, to whom he had been devoted.

Although E. B. generally preferred specie plants, he was particularly proud of a cross he created between yellow- and blue-flowering winter irises. He recorded the parents as *I. danfordiae* and *I. histrioides*, but the first parent is now thought to have been *I. winogradowii*. Named *Iris* 'Katherine Hodgkin' after the wife of his close friend Elliot Hodgkin, it was in any case an important breakthrough, for which he was awarded the Cory Cup in 1970.

Some nurseries stock a hebe to which Anderson's name has become spuriously attached. In his penultimate garden at West Porlock in Somerset there grew an unusual, purple-flowered variety now known to be *Hebe* 'Caledonia'. He had acquired it, nameless, from a friend in Scotland. E. B. reckoned that its attractively mauve-tinged leaves made it a small shrub worth growing for its winter foliage alone, and with his usual generosity he gave away many cuttings. Nameless plants seldom stay that way for long, and although investigation since has revealed its proper name to be *Hebe* 'Caledonia', it is still sometimes sold as *H.* 'E. B. Anderson'.

A cottage at Lower Slaughter became Anderson's home after the death of his wife. Here he had the smallest of the seven gardens, and so concentrated on alpines, his first love. It was during these last ten years that the Royal Horticultural Society asked him to write a book on Rock Gardens and another on Hardy Bulbs. Both of them are classics, being written with simplicity, wide knowledge and practical experience. He received numerous visitors, and, aged eighty-five, even went on a trip to the Dolomites, but shortly afterwards he became ill and died.

The wonderful collection of plants was distributed between his friends, amongst them alpine enthusiast and nurseryman Joe Elliott (*qv*). Anderson had grown a golden-leaved thyme, which he valued for bright winter colour. It also has growing tips in spring of a more pronounced red than the similar *Thymus citriodorus* 'Archer's Gold'. After his old friend's death, Elliott put it into commerce, calling it *T. citriodorus* 'Bertram Anderson'.

The naming of *Sedum* 'Bertram Anderson' came about in much the same way. Of unknown origin, this prostrate sedum, with small, red flowers, and mahogany-coloured leaves on trailing stems, was one of hundreds of treasures in the garden at Lower Slaughter. Anderson gave a piece to Joe Elliott, and later, when he began selling it commercially, *Sedum* 'Bertram Anderson' was the obvious name.

With his discerning eye, plants grown by Anderson were almost bound to be particularly choice. The *Pulmonaria longifolia* which bears his name was probably given to a friend—both its origin and naming remain obscure. A distinctive feature, however, is that the bright blue flowers are borne in a ball-like cluster. A modern plantswoman with a collection of pulmonaria, reports that when visitors see this particular plant flowering, it is the one everybody wants.

Despite introducing and breeding many new species and varieties over the years, it is an indication of E. B.'s innate modesty that only four plants now commemorate him or his wife, and they were named by friends.

E. B. Anderson

NORMAN HADDEN
1889–1971

Cornus 'Norman Hadden'
Cytisus 'Porlock'
Kniphofia 'Underway'
Mahonia × media 'Underway'
Rosmarinus officinalis 'Severn Sea'

At the end of the first world war a General and Mrs Hadden were advised that they should move from Aberdeen. Its climate was not suitable for their twenty-nine year old son Norman, who was in very poor health, and in order to give him a better chance of survival they moved to the Somerset village of West Porlock. Situated on the southern shore of the Bristol Channel, or Severn Sea, the area enjoys particularly mild winters.

Norman liked natural history and, inspired by an elderly neighbour, soon became interested in gardening. A shy and retiring bachelor, he devoted himself to his plants, and rented more and more land, ending up fifty years later with five separate gardens and a piece of woodland on a hillside some way from the house.

He loved to collect the rare and the beautiful and, owing to the mild microclimate around Porlock, was able to grow things which would not have been hardy further inland. His gardens were inspiring collections of plants and shrubs, rather than designed for artistic impact, and so many different species grew in close proximity that they frequently crossed, with exciting results.

One such offspring was a seedling that appeared in the garden about 1925, and was presumed to be a hybrid between sweet-scented *Genista fragrans* and the rather coarse *Cytisus monspessulanus*. Pleasingly fragrant and with the greater hardiness of the cytisus, it was, Hadden considered, a much better garden plant than either of its parents. He showed flowering branches of the hybrid at the Chelsea Show in 1931, where it received an Award of Merit.

The original shrub blew down in a storm, but seed from it came reasonably true, and Norman selected one seedling which had larger racemes than the original form. By 1941 the hybrid was already stocked by nurserymen, who called it the Porlock Broom.

120

Hadden thought this a pity, since it was not a broom in the ordinary sense but a genista, and nowadays nurseries list it as either *Genista* or *Cytisus* 'Porlock'.

'I have always been specially attracted by winter flowers, and have planted all I could find which flower between November and March', Norman Hadden recorded. He had a whole bed devoted to *Iris unguicularis*, and succeeded in his determination to have some species of cyclamen in flower every month of the year. Many winter-flowering shrubs were planted, and he had a collection of over 130 camellias, some imported direct from Japan via the trans-Siberian railway.

He also grew several varieties of mahonia. They seeded about with their usual abandon, and one seedling had attractive young foliage, a compact, dome-shaped habit and flowers of bright yellow in November and December. It became known as *Mahonia* 'Underway', after Hadden's house, which in turn had taken its name from The Underway, an ancient packhorse track which ran nearby.

An immensely shy man, Norman Hadden owed much to his brisk and devoted housekeeper for forty years, May Edwards, who insisted he be sociable when his natural inclinations were reclusive. As a result he counted great gardeners such as E. B. Anderson (*qv*) (who became a neighbour), Arthur Hillier and Margery Fish amongst his many gardening friends, and he was a great influence on the Heathcoat Amorys when they were developing their garden at Knightshayes in Devon.

'It is always encouraging to find one's plants reproducing themselves naturally, as it shows they have made themselves at home', Hadden remarked, and in 1958 he noted a seedling under an American dogwood, *Cornus nuttallii*, which seemed to be a cross with nearby *C. kousa*.

In early summer the new, semi-evergreen shrub was studded with a mass of star-shaped white flowers turning to pink, and in autumn it bore a lovely crop of red fruits. Cuttings were given to Hillier's Nursery and to Lady Anne Palmer of Rosemoor, and the shrub was exhibited in 1968 as *Cornus* 'Porlock'.

At about that time another cornus seedling was found at Underway. This was given to Lady Heathcoat Amory for the garden at Knightshayes, and in 1974 she exhibited it as *Cornus* 'Norman Hadden'. Its characteristics were very similar to *C*. 'Porlock', which caused confusion, and in addition botanists were beginning to question the origin of *Cornus* 'Porlock'. Recently the parentage of both seedlings has been established as evergreen *Cornus capitata* and *C. kousa*.

Some controversy now also surrounds *Kniphofia* 'Underway'. Before the war Hadden sowed a batch of seeds from the orange *K. galpinii*, resulting in a great variety of shades of orange, lemon, and even a white one. 'The best of these seedlings', he reported, 'is a very showy orange form of medium height which makes a wonderful display in October, being exceptionally free-flowering. It has very narrow bright green leaves, and has been named "Underway".' With his usual generosity he gave offsets away but plants now sold as *Kniphofia* 'Underway' do not always match his original description.

Probably the most well known plant to come from Norman Hadden's garden is the dark-flowered *Rosmarinus officinalis* 'Severn Sea'. All the plants now sold originated from one seedling which Hadden noticed at Paignton Zoo one day in the 1950's. He was particularly interested in rosemaries with strong blue flowers, and begged the seedling from his friend Herbert Whitley (*qv*), the zoo's owner. When the plant grew, Hadden was so pleased with its qualities that initially he was unwilling to give away cuttings. Having fine foliage, the rosemary grows some 3ft (90cm) high, with spreading, semi-prostrate branches. In West Porlock's mild climate it was long-lived, but none of the dark-flowered rosemaries are particularly hardy, and it is wise to take cuttings of *R.o.* 'Severn Sea' in case of a really hard winter.

Hadden was awarded the Victoria Medal of Honour by the Royal Horticultural Society in 1963. He died eight years later, aged eighty-one, leaving the house and garden to May Edwards, who did not long survive him. Fortunately, before her death she was wise enough to give away to gardening friends many of his treasures, and although the garden at Underway is a plantsman's paradise no more, Norman Hadden and his wonderful collection of plants have left the gardening world enriched.

SIR CEDRIC MORRIS
1889–1982

Dianthus 'Cedric's Oldest'
Iris 'Benton Arundel'
Iris 'Benton Cordelia'
Iris 'Benton Dierdre'
Iris 'Benton Farewell'
Iris 'Benton Lorna'
Iris 'Benton Nigel'
Iris 'Benton Sheila'
Narcissus minor 'Cedric Morris'
Papaver orientale 'Cedric's Pink'
Rose 'Sir Cedric Morris'

Flowers named after the artist Sir Cedric Morris commemorate a man who was as passionate about plants as he was about painting. From 1940 until his death, Morris and his friend Arthur Lett-Haines ran their highly individual East Anglian School of Painting and Drawing from Benton End, a rambling old house at Hadleigh in Suffolk. Always full of stimulating talk and company. Benton End became a Mecca for painters and gardeners alike.

Papaver orientalis 'Cedric's Pink' was a seedling that appeared in the garden bearing a rather smoky pink flower. It was eventually marketed by nurserywoman Beth Chatto, for whom Cedric Morris was both inspiration and mentor, as he was to a wide circle of gardening friends, all encouraged to visit whenever they liked. Cedric Morris saw himself as a link in a chain of gardeners who would learn and in turn pass on their knowledge, and he was unfailingly generous both with time and plants.

In his younger years he travelled almost every winter to places like Portugal and Turkey, living cheaply, painting, and collecting plants, and he was responsible for bringing back from the Mediterranean many fritillaries and other bulbs not previously grown in gardens. The yellow miniature narcissus which bears his name comes from the Costa Verde in Northern Spain. A friend driving down to meet Cedric dug up some bulbs by the roadside. They flourished in the dry, light soil at Benton End, usually flowering for Christmas, and some bulbs were given to Beth Chatto who now sells just a few each year. A subsequent visit to the site in Spain revealed that the road had been widened and the colony of narcissus was no more.

Cedric's walled garden was informal, with plants put first and the arrangement of the garden second. The artist Lucien Freud, a former pupil, remarked that at first the garden seemed rather a mess, but the more you looked the more interesting it became, at all seasons.

It was full of things which had seeded themselves, often helped by Cedric who, if he wanted to increase stock, would simply scatter seed around the parent plant. One year a vigorous seedling rose appeared, with leaves and young shoots of a glaucous purple and clusters of fragrant, white, single flowers. Probably a cross between *Rosa rubrifolia* and *R. mulliganii*, it was enjoyed quietly by Cedric for about ten years, and then a friend persuaded the rose nurseryman Peter Beales to come and see it. He thought it an outstanding rose, took cuttings and named it 'Sir Cedric Morris'.

One day when visiting Manningtree in Essex, Cedric saw a double pink in a cottage garden, begged a cutting and established it at Benton End. He was convinced it was very old and passed on cuttings to friends, one of whom described it as 'like raspberry mousse when you've put the cream in but not stirred it much'. After Morris's death a name had to be found for this pink, and it is now commercially available as *Dianthus* 'Cedric's Oldest'.

Cedric Morris had rude things to say about magenta, preferring the same off-beat colours in flowers that he used in his paintings. By a long process of selection he produced the range of grey, mauve and smokey-white *Papaver rhoeas* marketed for the first time in 1987 by Thompson and Morgan as 'Fairy Wings' but known in all his friends' gardens as 'Cedric's Poppies'.

Although he mostly preferred specie plants, at different times in the forty years at Benton End irises, lilies and old roses were particular enthusiasms. He was the first to produce a pink iris, named *I.* 'Edward Windsor', Cedric being a great admirer of the then Prince of Wales. Most of the irises he bred and registered in the forties and fifties however bore the prefix 'Benton'. Many are still highly regarded, and soft mauve 'Benton Cordelia' was the first variety to receive the British Iris Society's Silver Medal at its initial showing.

In his will Cedric left all the plants at Benton End to a friend, Jenny Robinson, knowing that she would organise their dispersal to the specialist societies; to Wisley; and his gardening friends, and this was done. The Secretary of the Iris Society was invited to take back seedling irises, and among them was an outstanding blue flower with darker falls which the Society registered and named. They called it *Iris* 'Benton Farewell'.

Sir Cedric Morris

LODDON NURSERY AND THOMAS CARLILE
1890–1957

Anchusa 'Loddon Royalist'
Campanula lactiflora 'Loddon Anna'
Delphinium belladonna 'Wendy'
Helianthus decapetalus 'Loddon Gold'
Heliopsis scabra 'Light of Loddon'
Lavandula 'Loddon Pink'
Monarda 'Loddon Crown'
Solidago 'Loddon Gold'
Veronica prostrata 'Loddon Blue'
Veronica spicata incana 'Wendy'

The River Loddon is a tributary of the Thames, joining it just North of Twyford in Berkshire, and it was beside the Loddon at Twyford that Tommy Carlile bought seven acres of land in 1920 to start a nursery. Aged thirty, he had already had fifteen years' experience working for other nurseries, including Waterer's and Perry's (*qv*), with whom he helped exhibit at the first Chelsea Flower Show in 1912.

For his own nursery he laid out broad walks and planted hedges of yew and beech. These looked attractive as well as being wind-breaks, and fronting the main road to Henley he made two enormous borders. Delphiniums were an early speciality, and one summer he filled these beds with 22,000 delphiniums, a magnificent spectacle which passing motorists could hardly fail to notice.

Tommy Carlile's ambition was to have one of the most comprehensive collections of hardy plants and alpines in the country, and he was always on the look out for good new plants. One of his earliest triumphs was *Helianthus decapetalus* 'Loddon Gold'. A wild flower of the United States, the single form of this tall, rather coarse yellow daisy is not a choice garden plant, but by 1924 Carlile's had produced one with big double flowers. *Helianthus decapetalus* 'Loddon Gold' was a dramatic improvement on all previous varieties, and earned the nursery one of its first Awards of Merit from the Royal Horticultural Society.

'I might be permitted to state here that I believe my stock contains a greater variety of Award of Merit plants than that of any other nursery during the same period', Tommy Carlile declared proudly in his catalogue, from which customers could select 'The Thousand and One Best Plants of 1925'

Tommy lived on the nursery with his wife and two daughters, Iris and Wendy, and his knowledge, hard work and enthusiasm brought success. By 1934 the nursery had expanded to take in all four corners of the crossroads where the A321 met the Great West Road. Dazzling roadside displays of flowers were bound to catch the eye, and a large board announcing the nursery's name caused speeding motorists to call it 'Charley's Corner'. To those going slow enough to read the board properly, the junction became 'Carlile's Corner', and it has remained so ever since.

Delphiniums were fashionable and in great demand in the 1930's. Hundreds of new ones were named—Loddon Nursery alone stocked 500 varieties. Very few have survived, but a choice delphinium which Tommy Carlile named in 1932 after his younger daughter is still popular. *Delphinium belladonna* 'Wendy' has spikes of cobalt blue flecked with purple, and a blue and white eye. Only 3ft (91cm) high, its sturdy habit makes it particularly valuable for today's smaller gardens.

Wendy inherited her father's love of plants, and joined the business when she grew up, but as a small child she had a patch of her own on which to grow whatever she wanted. One day she drew Tommy's attention to a flower she had grown—'Look Daddy, that's an odd one'. It was a *Campanula lactiflora*, but instead of the usual blue flowers, this one plant had blooms of a muted pink. Years were required to build up stocks, and by 1952 when Carlile's launched it, Tommy's daughter Iris had just given him a grandchild, Anna. *Campanula lactiflora* 'Loddon Anna' can grow to 5ft (150cm), and in late summer the big, branched heads of pale pink bell-flowers make a striking sight at the back of a border. It has become probably the nursery's most famous plant.

Tommy Carlile's whole life was bound up with plants, and his expertise was legendary. He served on many judging committees, and if he said a plant was 'No damn good', it was no good. He had an eye for plants second to none, plus a phenomenal memory, so that other nurserymen always turned to him for information about a plant. His enthusiasm, good humour and zest for life made him friends everywhere, and he was a wonderful raconteur. Vivid stories were always enhanced by expansive gestures, but to the alarm of his friends, he would often launch into some yarn while driving. People living on the road between Twyford Station and the nursery soon learnt to recognise the sound of Tommy's approaching three and a half litre BSA, and get out of the way smartly.

Soil at the nursery was very light, and thus well-suited to lavenders, of which Carlile's grew enormous quantities. In 1946 they exhibited a new one, *Lavandula* 'Loddon Pink', which with its compact habit and muted, greyish-pink flowers gives a wonderfully subtle note to garden colour schemes, and it has been a steady seller ever since.

Subtlety is not one of the qualities of *Anchusa azurea* 'Loddon Royalist', but it is an excellent border plant—in Tommy Carlile's opinion the best he ever introduced. With his unerring eye for something special, he picked one seedling out of the box sent by nurserymen Watkins and Simpson of West London, and grew it on. There were already several varieties of *Anchusa azurea* available, in different shades of blue, but growth tended to be straggly so that they had to be staked. This plant had a much more compact habit, and panicles of large flowers in gentian blue. It also bloomed right through from May to July. Tommy Carlile exhibited his new plant at the Chelsea Show in 1957, and was delighted that it received an Award of Merit. His pleasure had an added piquancy, for he had been suffering from cancer for some time, and knew that Chelsea would be his last.

He died three months later, mourned by everyone who had known this immensely likeable man. 'It doesn't matter what you do in Life, as long as you do it well', his daughters were always told, and Tommy Carlile lived up to his own maxim.

Carlile's Corner has become a roundabout, but more than thirty years later the nursery run by Wendy and her husband still supplies a range of hardy plants to the gardening public.

HEADBOURNE HYBRIDS
AND THE HON LEWIS
PALMER
1894–1971

Agapanthus 'Headbourne Hybrids'

Agapanthus, the 'African Lily', was for years regarded as an exotic, tender plant. A photograph of Miss Ellen Willmott's Warley Place (*qv*) in late summer shows eight huge tubs of agapanthus in front of the house, a popular way of growing them, as they could be moved into a heated greenhouse before the frosts. Only in very mild areas were they planted in the garden.

At the end of the nineteenth century, however, a much hardier variety called *Agapanthus mooreanus* began to appear in Irish and English gardens, the source being Dublin's Glasnevin Botanic Garden. In the late 1930's a plant of this hardy agapanthus was given to the Honourable Lewis Palmer for his Hampshire garden.

Younger son of the second Earl of Selbourne, Lewis Palmer was an enthusiastic and very knowledgeable gardener, a friend of the great E. A. Bowles (*qv*). They shared a scholarly approach to plants and gardening, and Palmer was both impressed and intrigued by this hardy agapanthus, which survived the fierce winters of 1940 and 1941 completely unscathed. The puzzle increased when he discovered that there was no such named plant in the wild, and *Agapanthus umbellatus*, the name given to the tender species, was also invalid. Palmer had spent part of his childhood in South Africa, and immediately after the war happened to have business there, so he determined to solve the mystery.

The genus Agapanthus is confined to South Africa, with over ten different species native to the coast and the Drakensburg Mountains. The species growing near the sea, he ascertained, have broad, evergreen leaves, and are generally tender or half-hardy. As the Dutch colonised coastal areas first, these were the agapanthus sent to Europe at the end of the seventeenth century, establishing their reputation for tenderness. The species which grow in the mountains however, have a deciduous or herbaceous habit, enabling them to survive the frosts of winter safely underground. *Agapanthus moor-eanus* which had been sent to Glasnevin was, it appeared, a hybrid.

Lewis Palmer visited South Africa's Kirstenbosch Botanic Garden, and was shown the order beds, where all the known wild forms of agapanthus were grown, side by side. He asked for, and was willingly given, seed of the most beautiful.

Back in Hampshire, now in a new garden at Headbourne Worthy, Palmer sowed the seeds, and raised some 300 plants, carefully labelled according to the name on the seed packet. As each one grew and flowered, however, the realisation came that things were not entirely straightforward. 'They are fine garden plants', he recorded, 'but in the whole lot I would not venture to state that one single one was the legitimate child of its mother. What I have got is a tremendous variety of hybrids'. Obviously aga-panthus species interbred with alacrity, and as all the known species were grown close together at Kirstenbosch, they had made the most of the opportunity.

The flowers of the seedlings varied in colour from indigo-violet through all shades of blue to white, and in height from 1ft (30cm) to 4½ft (136cm). Leaves varied in width, the flowers differed in shape and number, and some began flowering in July while others waited until late September.

Over the next few years Palmer grew his hybrids on, noting the differences, picking out the best and sowing their seed. Some retained the deciduous habit of their high veldt ancestors, the foliage yellowing and dying in the autumn, but the leaves of most remained green and active until cut down by the frost. Despite this, he explained, almost all 'have inherited enough of the stamina of their upland parents not to take any serious damage from this frosting, and they come up next season as vigorous as ever and flower profusely'.

Some of the agapanthus were given names. Although few of these varieties are available today, 'Snowy Owl' and 'Victoria' were outstandingly good plants with white flowers; 'Cherry Holley' was a deep blue, and Lewis's daughter Penelope Palmer was commemo-rated by one that was particularly tall, and straight. A friend called a light blue that he was given, 'Luly', the soubriquet of its raiser; while the nurseryman Roland Jackson, who was given seed, named one resultant plant 'Dorothy Palmer', to honour Lewis's wife. She was a member of the Loder family, creators of famous gardens at Leonardslee and Wakehurst, and shared Lewis's passion for gardening. In contrast to his learned, scientific approach, she leaned more towards its artistic side.

When, in 1972, the Royal Horticultural Society began five-year trials of agapanthus, of the seventy-two entries at least sixty were the direct work of Lewis Palmer. Many more were selections from plants and seeds he had presented to nurserymen and friends, and as he gave these away unnamed, they became known as *Agapanthus* 'Headbourne Hybrids'.

Although agapanthus were a special interest, Palmer's garden held a rich variety of plants, despite being on chalk, and facing north. He bred and exhibited in 1947 a beautiful new hybrid philadelphus, called 'Beauclerk'. 'When the wind is setting slightly from the south-west', he remarked, 'the fragrance from the original plant drifts down through the garden in the evening'. Free-flowering, and with just a hint of purple at the base of each petal, this philadelphus is still regarded as one of the best.

Palmer bred lilies, had extensive collections of snowdrops and hellebores, and was particularly fond of small bulbs, for which he made a large scree bed. On the genus cyclamen he was an acknowledged authority. Sir George Taylor, Director of Kew, once introduced him as 'the most knowledgeable botanical horticulturist whose friendship I can claim'. A Royal Horticultural Society Committee member for thirty years, Palmer was an expert judge, and served as Treasurer of the Society from 1953 to 1965. In 1968 he resigned his appointments, having decided to move to Guernsey. There he could grow not only dwarf bulbs, but tender plants that would not have thrived at Headbourne. He died three years later, aged seventy-seven.

Nowadays if you buy an agapanthus labelled 'Headbourne Hybrid' there is no certainty as to what colour, height or flowering season the plant will have. But it will be hardy, and for these good-tempered perennials which give a welcome touch of blue in late summer, modern gardeners owe a debt of gratitude to the enquiring mind and patience of the Hon Lewis Palmer.

DOROTHY PERKINS
?–1968

Rose 'Dorothy Perkins'

If Christopher Robin Milne felt burdened by the stories and poems his father wrote about him as a child, Dorothy Perkins, after whom possibly the most famous of all roses was named, would probably have sympathised.

It was 1873 when one Charles H. Perkins first went into market gardening with his father-in-law Albert Jackson, at Newark near Lake Ontario in North America. Grapes and raspberries were their first speciality, but the business prospered, and widened in scope to include roses. Customers liked buying from Charlie Perkins, who would tell them, 'If it doesn't grow for you, let me know', promising a refund or a replacement rose. In 1884 he took on a young man named Alvin Miller to do research.

At this time nurserymen were finding that many of the roses bred in Europe were unsuitable for the harsh winters of North East America. In 1888 a German nursery sent plants of *Rosa wichuraiana*, a species from East China, to the Arnold Arboretum in Massachusetts. Besides having attractive, glossy leaves that in suitable conditions remained all winter, this wild rose had a rambling, ground-covering habit, putting out long shoots which rooted as they grew. It was also extremely hardy, and several American nurseries began to use it in experimental breeding.

By 1897 a nurseryman named W. A. Manda of New Jersey had produced several 'Wichuraiana Hybrids', with bold names such as 'Manda's Triumph' and (hopefully) 'Universal Favourite'. They attracted brief notice, and other nurseries soon followed.

Alvin Miller of Jackson and Perkins tried his hand, and in one of his experiments crossed *R. wichuraiana* with a French rose, 'Madame Gabriel Luizet'. The result was a hybrid with a climbing habit, bright green leaves, great clusters of double, strong pink flowers, and a good fragrance. By the turn of the century Charles Perkins' son George had joined the firm, and when they launched their rose in 1901, it was named after George's young daughter, Dorothy.

The new rose caused much favourable comment at a Pan-

American Exhibition held shortly afterwards, and it was soon being grown in England. An amateur from Kent exhibited 'Dorothy Perkins' at the Royal Horticultural Society in 1902, where it was received with enthusiasm. 'Warm pink flowers almost as big as a crown piece; a splendid Rose for rafters and pergolas', was the verdict, and unanimously the judges voted it an Award of Merit.

The new Wichuraiana Hybrids had a great deal to recommend them, and were particularly suitable for training up the pillars and rose arches which were then in vogue. Soon no rose walk was complete without 'Dorothy Perkins'. She was all the rage.

By definition, something cannot be fashionable for very long, and as soon as it is seen everywhere, a plant becomes 'common'. 'Dorothy Perkins' was in 1918 already being dismissed by a member of the gardening elite as 'ubiquitous, and a rose frequently blighted by mildew'. Eleven years later, when Garden Cities were the current town planning enthusiasm, the distinguished gardening writer Clarence Elliott (*qv*) mused mischievously, 'I suppose some day in the dim future a last lost plant of "Dorothy Perkins" will be discovered in the ancient city of Letchworth, and revived and acclaimed as a quaint and fascinating treasure. But today there are gardeners who would gladly burn the last plant of Dorothy'.

Back in America, Jackson and Perkins continued to expand. A visitor to Newark in 1932 commented that the whole town seemed to belong to the firm. They began selling roses by mail order, which was then a great novelty, and became the largest rose grower in the world. From its present day base in California, Jackson and Perkins send out to customers some four million roses a year.

The Perkins family sold their interest in the firm in the 1960's, by which time Dorothy Perkins herself had long since retired gratefully into obscurity, by becoming Mrs E. P. Estabrooke, and is believed to have died in 1968. Perhaps she persuaded her father not to name any more roses after members of the family. The floribunda rose 'Ma Perkins', which Jackson and Perkins introduced in 1962, was called, not after a relation, but an American broadcaster who was well-known for her homely stories.

The name of Dorothy Perkins has endured, however. In 1909 a warehousing and drapery business called N. P. Newman Ltd started up in London. Seven years later, when everyone was planting the rose, the wife of Newman's Director suggested opening a shop, at Wood Green in North London, called 'Dorothy Perkins'.

Today there are some 300 branches of 'Dorothy Perkins' shops in

Britain. And the rose itself has proved nigh on indestructible. Grown on its own vigorous roots, it never goes to briar, and the loud pink blooms will appear happily year after year with no attention at all. There are undoubtedly quite a number still growing in Letchworth.

Rose 'Dorothy Perkins'

VERA JAMESON
1899–1989

Sedum 'Vera Jameson'

Vera Jameson lived at Doddington, in Gloucestershire, not far away from Norah Leigh (*qv*). Married into the Jameson whisky family, Vera was a keen plantswoman who grew many rare and beautiful plants in her 1½ acre garden.

She had several varieties of sedum, including *Sedum cauticolum*. This pink-flowered plant from coastal Japan is low-growing, with fleshy, glaucous green leaves tinged with red. She also grew the hybrid *Sedum* 'Ruby Glow', with pinky-mauve leaves and ruby flowers. In a bed not far away was one from Europe, *Sedum telephium maximum* Atropurpureum. A herbaceous perennial, growing some 2ft (60cm) high, this magnificent form has mahogany-dark leaves and stalks, and dusky red flowers. It does sometimes seed itself, the young plants usually coming true, and in about 1968 Mrs Jameson found a dark-leaved seedling in the garden.

When this grew she discovered the seedling had the low-growing habit of *Sedum cauticolum* or *S.* 'Ruby Glow', but that the lax foliage was bluey-purple, and in late summer it bore flat heads of smokey-pink flowers. The plant was most attractive, and realising that it could be something special, she asked Norah Leigh's nursery-man son-in-law, Joe Elliott (*qv*) to look at it.

He agreed with Mrs Jameson that the chance seedling had some very good properties, and she immediately gave him an offshoot. In 1971 he exhibited the new plant at a Royal Horticultural Society Show, under the name *Sedum* 'Vera Jameson'. It gained an Award of Merit, and seven years later, after trials at Wisley, a First Class Certificate. Since then it has become more widely grown every year, for to see this plant, giving a striking display after even the hottest summer, is to covet it.

Experts have since debated the exact parentage of *Sedum* 'Vera Jameson', but she herself was convinced that it was *S.* 'Ruby Glow' with *S. telephium maximum* 'Atropurpureum'. She was delighted to have the hybrid named after her, and pleased with its subsequent success. Although crippled with arthritis in later years and unable to garden, she remained at her Doddington house, spirited and mentally alert up to her death at the age of ninety.

ESTHER READ
1899–1991

Leucanthemum × *superbum* 'Esther Read'

We owe the creation of this much-loved border plant to the leisurely pace of a Great Eastern Railway train. In the 1920's country trains slowed frequently to take on water or throw off newspapers and mail, and one day Horace Read, a Norfolk nurseryman, was travelling by train to Great Yarmouth for the day. As it slowed, he spotted on the embankment a semi-double ox-eye daisy, *Chrysanthemum leucanthemum* (now renamed *Leucanthemum vulgare*). The Read family had been plantsmen for 200 years, and Horace was already a plant breeder of note, so while in Yarmouth he thought about it and decided the chance was too good to miss. On the way back he pulled the communication chord, whipped out and dug up the plant. History does not record whether or not he had to pay a fine, but *Leucanthemum* 'Esther Read' was the eventual outcome.

Many years of experimental breeding ensued, using the offspring of his find and the bigger *Chrysanthemum maximum*, and in 1931 he proudly exhibited the new flower, 'Esther Read', a white daisy with large, fully double blooms. Named after his daughter, the newcomer was an immediate success. This was still the age of big herbaceous borders, and with a long flowering season and height of only 18in (46cm), 'Esther Read' was in great demand as a front of the border plant. It was also excellent for cutting, and nurseries supplying the large cut flower market soon grew it extensively. Had there been a system for patenting new plants it would have made a fortune, but there were soon many imitators. Indeed when, in the 1980's, the present day Reads Nursery tried to obtain plants of *Leucanthemum* 'Esther Read' they had difficulty finding the true strain.

'Esther Read' is not particularly hardy and tends to flower in flushes, so Horace Read went on experimenting in an effort to improve the strain. He launched a new variety named after himself, and later one honouring Pauline Read, his granddaughter, but they were not a great success.

In the 1950's a nephew, who also ran a nursery, bred a more

robust strain called *Leucanthemum* 'Jennifer Read', which had bold flowers on strong stalks. It was a great improvement on 'Esther Read', but created scarcely a ripple of interest, and is today not even commercially available. Times had changed. There were no longer so many labour-intensive herbaceous borders, while the cut flower trade had not only diminished but turned to more exotic blooms.

Leucanthemum 'Esther Read' had been the right flower at the right time to take the gardening world by storm. Indeed to many people white, low-growing, double border daisies are still quite simply, 'Esther Reads'.

Leucanthemum x superbum 'Esther Read'

STUART BOOTHMAN
1906–1976

Dicentra formosa 'Stuart Boothman'
Phlox douglasii 'Boothman's'
Primula × *pubescens* 'Boothman's Variety'

Stuart Boothman started his working life in banking and hated it. When he was twenty-one, however, a legacy set him free to study horticulture, and in due course he joined the workforce of Walter Ingwersen's alpine plant nursery in Sussex.

The bluff young man from Lancashire was fascinated by the variety and beauty of the plants grown by Ingwersens, and when in 1933 he was able to set up his own nursery it specialised, unsurprisingly, in alpines.

At Nightingale Nursery, Furze Platt, near Maidenhead, Boothman built up a thriving business in mail order, issuing a comprehensive catalogue of plants which were described with enthusiasm, and a pleasing dash of humour. His terms of business were in advance of the time too. 'Please note how favourable they are in comparison with other firms', he suggested boldly. Confident in the health of his stock and his own skilful packing, he guaranteed to replace any plants which died within six months of purchase. Such unorthodoxy was not perhaps a recipe for popularity with other nurserymen, but it encouraged customers, who also found it difficult to resist his yearly Bargain List of a dozen specified plants for nine shillings.

Boothman aimed to stock the best alpines, and the dwarf phlox which bears his name certainly comes into that category. Probably a chance seedling, it is showy, hardy and easy to grow. 'My form of *Phlox douglasii* is such a bright and cheerful version of the type that it has been given a varietal name', he announced in 1951. 'Instead of the usual washy lavender flowers this form has clear mauve petals with a vivid, violet-purple middle'.

He was pleased too with a dicentra that had 'silver leaves and dusky-red lockets in Spring'. It was a rare plant, he said, and described it in 1963 as *Dicentra oregana rosea*. The dicentra from Oregan is not now considered to be a distinct species, and experts are divided as to whether *Dicentra* 'Stuart Boothman' is a form of *D. eximia* or *D. formosa*. Since the two hybridise easily, and

Boothman's was almost certainly a chance seedling, the argument probably has many years to run. Whatever its parentage, the plant is a real treasure, with finely-divided glaucous leaves making a silvery-bronze background for the deep pink flowers.

Stuart Boothman grew many alpine primulas, and another of his selections has stood the test of time. The parentage of *Primula* × *pubescens* 'Boothman's Variety' is also obscure, but it has dark, reddish purple flowers, some 4in (10cm) high. Being particularly vigorous and easy to grow—qualities notably absent from many alpines—the plant's popularity seems assured.

For over thirty years Stuart Boothman lived at the nursery with his family, during which time it became a magnet for alpine plant enthusiasts. He built up a gardening library housed in an old shed, and beside it stood a venerable quince tree on which mistletoe had been persuaded to grow. Visitors liked the nursery's informality and its forthright owner, and when he closed Nightingale Nursery, in 1970, following the death of his wife, it was a sad day.

Stuart Boothman subsequently moved to Wales, and died there in 1976.

Phlox douglasii 'Boothman's'

CLIVE GREAVES

Scabiosa caucasia 'Clive Greaves'

Between the wars, before florists began tempting customers with more exotic blooms, Caucasian scabious were widely grown for the British cut flower market. Long-stemmed and flowering for months on end, they are ideal for cutting.

Isaac House was a strawberry grower and market gardener at Westbury-on-Trym, near Bristol. In the 1920's, when his son James Clutterbuck House ran the business, Isaac House & Son began growing hardy plants. They still sold fruit, vegetables and cut flowers to the Bristol shops however, and for cutting the nursery grew *Scabiosa caucasia*. Strong blue flowers were most popular, and it was probably a quest for even darker colours which prompted James House to sow seed and begin breeding better varieties himself.

He did succeed in producing a deep purple variety, *Scabiosa caucasia* 'Isaac House', but it proved to have a weak constitution, as did another, called 'Harold' after his son. One great success was a pure white which he named 'Miss Willmott' in honour of Ellen Willmott (*qv*), a famous, and extravagant, gardener of the day. Nurserymen with impressive new cultivars found such moves were seldom bad for business.

The breeding programme continued, in a quest for deep blues, whites and anything with a hint of pink. One seedling with ordinary lavender-blue flowers, produced in the 1920's, seemed unexciting, but the blooms were well-shaped and prolific, so it was kept.

At that time a young man named Clive Greaves was a salesman for Hewitts Nursery at Solihull, his work taking him round a good few nurseries. Meeting James House at a flower show one year, Greaves, who was not lacking in confidence, suggested that if a scabious were named after him he would be able to sell it in large quantities. Accordingly this apparently very ordinary seedling became *Scabiosa caucasia* 'Clive Greaves'. No-one had any idea that over the years it would out-perform all the others in productivity and reliability.

A further irony was that even had the plant been as average as he thought, James House would never have called it 'Clive Greaves' if he had known more about the young man himself. House was something of a puritan, teetotal and highly religious, while by contrast Clive Greaves had a weakness for women and wine.

Scabiosa caucasia 'Clive Greaves' may owe it's success in part to the salesmanship of its namesake, but the plant is certainly outstanding in its strong constitution and prolific flowering. Isaac House and Son went on growing and breeding scabious for another thirty years, until the nursery was sold for development, but they never succeeded in bettering the plant named just to humour the young salesman at a flower show.

Scabiosa caucasia 'Clive Greaves'

BAGGESEN'S NURSERY

Chamaecyparis lawsoniana 'Pembury Blue'
Lonicera nitida 'Baggesen's Gold'

Niels Baggesen came to England from Denmark at the end of the last century, and worked at Kew Gardens before starting up a small nursery of his own near Cardiff. Just before the Second World War he moved to Pembury in Kent, and set up Baggesen's Nursery, his two sons Harald and John later joining him in the business. Baggesens of Pembury had a succession of premises, but for almost thirty years the firm sold shrubs, trees, and roses, as well as engaging in landscaping work.

As their father grew older, Harald Baggesen specialised more in the landscape side of the nursery, while John organised the growing of stock. He liked to take customers round personally, and was always happy to discuss the merits and drawbacks of different varieties, whether or not people eventually bought plants. He budded the roses and propagated trees and shrubs himself, always keeping a sharp eye open for mutations or sports that could be used to form a new variety.

The Lawson cypress, *Chamaecyparis lawsoniana*, was introduced from America in 1854, and has since given rise to nearly a hundred different cultivars, so prone is it to mutations. A few years after the war John Baggesen spotted a sport with dove-grey foliage. He propagated it successfully, and in 1950 exhibited the young tree at the Royal Horticultural Society, under the name *Chamaecyparis lawsoniana* 'Pembury Blue'. To his disappointment the judges did not consider it worth an award. Neither was the new variety a commercial success for Baggesens, and it was only when Jackmans Nursery of Woking included it in their catalogue, eleven years later, that the good qualities of *C.l.* 'Pembury Blue' began to be noticed.

Growing to quite a tall, conical tree, *C.l.* 'Pembury Blue' has young foliage of a unique, soft blue-grey. No other glaucous-leaved form can boast such a delicate shade, and nowadays it is generally acknowledged as the most outstanding blue cultivar.

Baggesens were unlucky with their introductions. Several new roses were developed, including one named 'John Baggesen', but they came to nothing. However the family reckoned they had a winner in waiting. In the early years of the war John had been excited to discover on a specimen of *Lonicera nitida*, a young shoot whose tip had golden leaves instead of the usual dark green. It measured only an inch or so, but with great care he propagated the sport and built up stock. His father was particularly enthusiastic, showing the new form to knowledgeable friends, and in 1952 the nursery exhibited it at a Royal Horticultural Society Show, as *Lonicera nitida* 'Baggesen's Gold'. Inexplicably, this eye-catching shrub was also passed over, gaining no award at all.

Increasingly since then Baggesen's golden-leaved lonicera has been used as a hedging plant throughout the country, its dense sprays of yellow leaves offering privacy as well as a change from the usual green. *Lonicera* 'Baggesen's Gold' is seen at its best however when grown as a specimen shrub, reaching some 10ft (3m) high, the arching branches bearing small, white, scented flowers followed by purple berries.

Unfortunately the shrub was never a money spinner for Baggesens. In common with many other nurseries, they struck hard times in the late 1960's, and eventually closed, their land being sold for development. John Baggesen died in 1985. He could justifiably have been bitter over the way the excellent plants he raised went initially unrecognised. He was however generous enough merely to take pleasure in their eventual success.

KOICHIRO WADA
1907–1981

Clematis 'Wada's Primrose'
Magnolia 'Wada's Memory'
Rhododendron yakushimanum 'Koichiro Wada'
Saxifraga cortusifolia fortunei 'Wada's Variety'

Scheduled airline services have now made intercontinental travel commonplace, but even today people would surely look askance at the idea of ordering plants from as far away as Japan. In the 1930's, however, gardeners could, and did, order choice shrubs such as magnolias, camellias, rhododendrons and tree peonies from a nursery near Yokohama. The plants travelled in coffin-like, ventilated boxes on the trans-Siberian railway, arriving with leaves rather blanched from lack of light, but perfectly sound.

The reason for the trade was an anglophile nurseryman named Koichiro Wada. His nursery, at Numazu, was beautifully situated between the sea and the foot of Mount Fuji, and besides selling, he was also dedicated to breeding better forms of plants, trees and shrubs, particularly rhododendrons. As a twelve year old he had tried unsuccessfully to grow rhododendrons, but instead of failure disheartening him, he became interested in the idea of breeding hardier ones.

Magnolias and pieris were also special enthusiasms, along with camellias. 'It is very rare that any plant can retain its top class position for a hundred years without being improved', he said, reminding people that the range of colours and forms in camellias was the result of a thousand years of improvement. He himself bred a number of new camellia varieties bearing Japanese names.

Wada visited Britain several times, making friends among many of the country's eminent gardeners, and he was delighted when able to return the hospitality. One English visitor toured his nursery and private garden, both full of interesting plants, and reported, 'It was a little embarrassing on my return home three months later to find awaiting me many plants I had admired in nursery and garden, accompanied by expressions of friendship'.

When it looked as if Japan would become involved in the Second World War, Koichiro Wada feared for his plants, and in 1940 he sent some of his most promising magnolia seed to the University of Washington Arboretum at Seattle. Of the seedlings that resulted, one particularly caught the Director's eye. It grew to a small, conical tree, covered in April with fragrant, white flowers. When their petals fluttered in the breeze the effect was of a myriad hovering butterflies. By this time there was a rumour in the gardening world that the donor of the seed had been killed, so the magnolia was named 'Wada's Memory'.

Suffering unpopularity and suspicion because of his pro-British sympathies, Wada did in fact survive the war. Sadly, his first wife and a son were killed, a tragedy about which he was forgivingly philosophical. Although working in Yokohama, he had managed to continue plant breeding. 'So far as the raising of new meritable plants are concerned, the past seven years were not wasted', he wrote to an English friend after the war. 'I have raised a wonderful strain of azaleas, a wonderful coloured rhododendron, a new hybrid magnolia, a hybrid hamamelis, many fine camellias, etc'.

Another of the plants that he sent abroad just before the war now bears his name. Two specimens of *Rhododendron yakushimanum* were sent to Exbury, near Southampton, the Rothschild's garden famous for its azalea and rhododendron collections. One of these two plants was taken to The Royal Horticultural Society's garden at Wisley, and in 1947 was awarded a First Class Certificate. The shrub grows wider than its 3ft (92cm) height, and in May pink buds open to bellshaped flowers of almost pure white. It has subsequently been used in the breeding of many good hybrids. This species of rhododendron comes from the most southerly island of Japan, and although the area has since been thoroughly combed for further plants, none have been found as good as the two Wada sent to Exbury.

Clematis patens is a variable species which is found throughout much of Japan, and *Clematis* 'Wada's Primrose' is thought to be a particularly good form, or possibly a hybrid. Its exact origin is unclear, but Koichiro Wada certainly introduced it to Europe. The flowers of palest yellow have an elegant simplicity but, being very prone to clematis wilt, it is not easy to grow.

Saxifraga cortusifolia fortunei is a much more robust garden plant, found in damp, shady places in both Japan and China. Flowering in October, one petal on each of its dainty, white flowers becomes curiously elongated, and the waxy leaves, green on top and pink-tinged underneath, make a handsome foil. Wada grew a form with attractive, red flower stalks, and leaves of shiny bronze on top with an undersurface of dark pink. He sent this form to customers and friends in Britain, and it became known as *Saxifraga fortunei* 'Wada's Variety' (botanists have now lengthened the name). There seems, however, little to choose between this and a similar coloured form called *Saxifraga cortusifolia fortunei* 'Rubrifolia'.

In 1965 the Royal Horticultural Society awarded Koichiro Wada an Honourary Fellowship, thought to be the first ever received by a citizen of Japan. 'Mr Wada', declared the President, 'with his Japanese rhododendrons and azaleas, his maples, his tree paeonies, above all the camellias that he has cultivated and introduced, has greatly added to the beauty to be found in British gardens'.

Wada had opened a nursery in Yokohama, where high summer temperatures tested the heat tolerance of his rhododendron hybrids, and another in the mountain area of Amagi, to test winter hardiness. He liked to live up there alone in a cottage, once his son took a hand in the business, and at the age of seventy he died. Today in Japan two Rhododendron Gardens have been opened, each containing over 5,000 hybrids bred by Koichiro Wada, a gentle, unassuming man who devoted a lifetime to breeding better plants.

Koichiro Wada

KEN ASLET
1909–1980

Oxalis purpurea 'Ken Aslet'
Tropaeolum tuberosum 'Ken Aslet'
Verbascum 'Letitia'

K en Aslet was a plantsman, botanist, nurseryman and a great character. He was held in much affection at Wisley, the Royal Horticultural Society's garden, where he worked in the Rock Garden Department for twenty-six years.

After studying horticulture at Reading, Aslet worked for several nurseries, including Carliles (*qv*), and Toynbee's of Bognor Regis (*qv*). In 1949 he joined Wisley as Foreman of the Rock Garden Department, becoming Superintendent twelve years later. Generations of students appreciated his knowledge, interest and discipline, and he supervised the major redevelopment of the Rock Garden in 1964. 'You really should come round in the winter sometimes to see what a right old mess we can make', he told Fellows of the Royal Horticultural Society cheerfully. He was never happier than when up to his elbows in mud, sorting out some problem connected with water flow, causing a friend at Wisley to dub him the Drain Brain.

Aslet was tremendously knowledgeable on herbs, trees, shrubs and wild flowers, as well as alpines, and he had a good eye for a plant. *Oxalis purpurea* 'Ken Aslet' is a particularly fine form of a South African alpine, which he selected at Wisley. With yellow flowers, and trifoliate leaves, grey above and purple underneath, it is a beautiful little plant, without the aggressive habits of so many of the oxalis family. However, being dormant from April to October and flowering in the winter, it is troubled by our wet weather and is best grown in an alpine house.

'Funny things can happen in our Alpine House', Ken Aslet observed, referring to the appearance at Wisley of the outstanding *Verbascum* 'Letitia'. Growing there in the late 1950's were *Verbascum spinosum*, a diminutive species from Crete, and *V. dummulosum*, which had been found thriving on the crumbling walls of ancient temples in Turkey. 'They never meet in Nature', Aslet said, 'but they did meet in our Alpine House. They must have liked each other very much, because the charming offspring *V.* 'Letitia' was the result'. It was however Ken Aslet who took the trouble to grow the seedling on, recognised that it was special, and named it after his beloved wife, Letty.

The new hybrid was a better plant than either of the parents. Low growing with velvety grey leaves, its spreading stems are covered for weeks in early summer with yellow flowers, each with a chestnut-brown blotch at the base. Furthermore, it has proved hardy enough to be grown outside in dry situations, and today is planted in the Rock Garden at Wisley.

Ken Aslet was remarkably uncommercial. If someone admired a plant and asked him about it, like as not he would give it away. Such generosity led to wide distribution of the plants which came to be named after him, particularly *Tropaeolum tuberosum* 'Ken Aslet', an early flowering form of this showy member of the nasturtium family.

Tropaeolum tuberosum comes from Bolivia and Peru, and has been known in this country since 1827. It is not really hardy however, and since it only begins to bear cascades of spurred, orange blooms in September, the flowering season is usually short. Just before the Second World War a Dutch nurseryman heard of an earlier flowering form in Scotland, but after the war there was no trace of it. Ken Aslet never bothered with records, but quite possibly the summer flowering *T. tuberosum* which he grew in his garden in the 1950's had found its way to him directly or indirectly from Scotland.

He gave generously to all those who admired it. It is an easy plant to distribute, forming as it does a large quantity of tubers near the surface, which need to be lifted in autumn and stored in frost-free conditions. The plant is grown as a food crop in South America, and guests invited to eat with Ken and Letty were sometimes startled to be offered cooked tropaeolum tubers instead of potatoes.

Ken Aslet retired from Wisley in 1976, and died only four years later, aged seventy-one, mourned by all those who had known this warm-hearted and highly individual gardener.

JOE ELLIOTT

Arenaria purpurascens 'Elliott's Variety'
Campanula glomerata 'Joan Elliott'
Campanula 'Joe Elliott'
Dianthus alpinus 'Joan's Blood'
Primula allionii 'Elliott's Variety'

Joe Elliott, son of Clarence Elliott of Six Hills Nursery (*qv*), trained at Six Hills and at Edinburgh Botanic Garden, and in 1946 he founded his own successful alpine nursery at Broadwell in the Cotswolds. A friend of E. B. Anderson (*qv*), and son-in-law of Norah Leigh (*qv*), Joe was responsible for introducing into commercial production a number of good plants, some of which bear his name.

The very first resulted from a plant-hunting trip to Northern Spain in 1930 when, in the Cantabrian Mountains, Joe and his father found *Arenaria purpurascens* growing plentifully. Despite its name, the star-shaped flowers of this ground-hugging little plant are usually a rather washy pink. Joe, however, came across one that was a much deeper colour, and in due course it was included in the Six Hills Nursery Catalogue as *A.p.* 'Elliott's Variety'.

Campanula 'Joe Elliott' is a chance cross, spotted in a tray of seedlings, between two European alpines, *Campanula raineri* and the difficult *C. morettiana*. Their offspring inherited good points from both parents, and in 1978 this hardy, long-flowering hybrid received the Royal Horticultural Society's Award of Merit.

Joe Elliott's own garden in the Cotswolds was the source of a strain of campanula which commemorates his wife, Joan. Nurseryman Alan Bloom of Bressingham was staying one weekend in May, when he spotted the purple flowers of *Campanula glomerata*. 'That shouldn't be flowering now, it's far too early', he observed. Joe had never given the plant's eagerness much thought but Alan Bloom duly went home with a clump, and within a couple of seasons it was offered as *Campanula glomerata* 'Joan Elliott'.

Mrs Elliott is also the Joan in the memorably named *Dianthus alpinus* 'Joan's Blood'. About 1955 she and her husband were surveying a batch of *Dianthus alpinus* seedlings. The plant is slightly variable both in the colour and in the amount of speckling in the centre of the petals, and Joan noticed a particularly striking one. She bent down to point it out with a finger scratched by a bramble, and her husband immediately remarked, 'It's exactly the same colour as your blood'. He took it into the alpine house and labelled it 'Joan's Blood' as a temporary measure, but the name stuck. The plant has bright red flowers above leaves of deep green which often take on a bronzy tint, and is reliably hardy, given sun and starvation.

Joe Elliott retired in due course, closing his nursery, but continues to take a keen interest in the growing and breeding of hardy plants, and alpines in particular.

PEGGY SAMMONS

Cistus 'Peggy Sammons'

The cistus family are a boon to gardeners with parched gardens and poor soil—although apt to be cursed after a severe winter has carried off the less hardy. In 1945 businessman J. E. Sammons and his wife Peggy went to live near Aldridge, some miles to the north of Birmingham, and at the top of their garden was a wide bank of stony subsoil. Just gorse flourished there, but it seemed a suitable site for cistus, and over the next few years he planted every variety he could obtain.

The result was not a great success. Many of them proved tender, or were damaged by wind and snow, and Mr Sammons decided to try breeding some himself. Initial results were, however, disappointing. Some of his plants had come from Ingwersen's Nursery in Sussex, and in 1953 a letter to them brought a helpful response from the firm's founder, Walter Ingwersen. He sent a booklet giving the relationship between the species along with the parentage of all the known hybrids. No longer working blind, Mr Sammons continued hybridising.

Tall *Cistus laurifolius*, with leathery, evergreen leaves and white, saucer-shaped flowers is considered to be the hardiest of all cistuses, but it has a stiff, ungainly habit. In 1954 Sammons used it to pollinate grey-leaved *Cistus albidus*, which has pink flowers. Unfortunately all the resulting seed capsules dropped off before the seed was ripe, and early crossings made the following year were equally unsuccessful. It seemed too few seeds were being formed, so the last two *Cistus albidus* flowers available that summer were pollinated very lightly with *Cistus laurifolius* pollen, and later fertilised again with their own pollen, which had been saved. Mr Sammons was never sure whether this affected the result, but although both pods eventually fell off, the seed inside was ripe enough to sow.

The majority of the seedlings were hybrids, but only one, with oval, grey-green leaves, showed particular promise. Planted in a sunny spot between two bay windows, three summers later it bloomed for the first time, bearing large flowers of soft pink, like *Cistus albidus*. By 1961 the plant was 7ft (2.1m) tall, and that summer bore some 3,000 flowers.

Cuttings were rooted, and, now officially named *Cistus* 'Peggy Sammons', one was planted in the Royal Horticultural Society's garden at Wisley. There it caused much favourable comment, and in 1963 Mr Sammons sent a plant to Ingwersens, who distributed it.

In under thirty years *C.* 'Peggy Sammons' has become one of the most widely grown cistus cultivars. From *C.* laurifolius it inherits hardiness, and with grey-green leaves, the hybrid is attractive all year round. However some of the original vigour seems to have been lost, and modern specimens generally only grow to about 3ft (1m).

At Aldridge experiments continued with cistus, and the closely related halimiums, producing two more good hybrids—*Cistus* 'Snow White' and the dark-eyed *Halimium* 'Susan'. Although now unable to garden actively, Mr Sammons remains intrigued by cistus and halimiums. 'They are', he remarks, 'a fascinating and beautiful family, yet quite unpredictable'.

Cistus 'Peggy Sammons'

'CROFTWAY NURSERY'

Chamaecyparis lawsoniana 'Croftway'
Monarda didyma 'Croftway Pink'
Sidalcea 'Croftway Red'

Just after the First World War the Government organised a Land Settlement Scheme at Barnham, near Bognor Regis in West Sussex, and one of the units was bought by a Frank Toynbee. He called it Croftway Nursery, after the name of his house, and began by growing soft fruit. He soon realised however, as this area of coast developed, that there was a strong local demand for shrubs, trees and herbaceous plants, as well as a landscape service. Soft fruit was therefore abandoned in favour of garden plants.

In the days before plastic containers transformed the nursery trade, herbaceous plants were left to flower in the summer, only being lifted for sale when growth had died down. As a result 'sports' or seedlings with outstanding characteristics could be more easily noted and developed. *Monarda didyma* 'Croftway Pink' was one of these, selected about 1932 for its rose-pink flowers instead of the usual red. It also proved to have a good, strong constitution and has become one of the stalwarts of the herbaceous border, valuable for its late summer colour, and even tolerating quite dry conditions.

The Second World War meant food production took priority, but in the years afterwards the business flourished. Now known as Toynbee's Nursery, it was among the first to stock the extraordinarily fast-growing x *Cupressocyparis leylandii*, selling enormous numbers to those impatient for privacy or a wind break. The nursery selected and sold quite a few conifer varieties of its own, and *Chamaecyparis lawsoniana* 'Croftway', more compact than most, is still available.

Toynbees prided themselves on providing service as opposed to mere selling. 'We offer advice and willing help *after* the sale, even where the smallest purchase is concerned', customers were assured. They could also wander along nearly half a mile of mixed borders, and peruse a catalogue containing over two thousand different varieties of plants, illustrated by talented schoolmaster turned horticultural photographer, Harry Smith. The nursery won gold medals for its exhibits at Chelsea, and produced numerous 'Croftway' cultivars ranging from aubrieta to a famous, pure yellow gaillardia. From those years however, only *Sidalcea* 'Croftway Red' a strong pinky-red variety, now remains.

Frank Toynbee retired in 1948, and with his son was eventually bought out, but the nursery continued, producing mostly trees and shrubs. In 1975, after nearly half a century of trading, Toynbees closed. The site continued as a nursery and, now thriving under new ownership, is once again producing cultivars named 'Croftway'.

Monarda didyma 'Croftway Pink'

LANGTREES AND DR ROGERSON
1926–1987

Brunnera macrophylla 'Langtrees'
Dicentra 'Langtrees'
Francoa sonchifolia 'Rogerson's Form'
Osteospernum 'Langtrees'

Plants with 'Langtrees' after their Latin names came from Croyde in North Devon. In 1964 Dr Anthony Rogerson and his wife Marney bought a house there called Langtrees, and started a garden in what had been an old orchard. Some of the apple trees were left to give depth, as well as support for climbing plants, and the Rogersons created a sunken garden round the house, with a southern aspect so that semi-tropical plants could be grown against the house wall. The subsoil from this was used to make a high perimeter bank planted as a windbreak, since the garden took the full force of the salt-laden wind off the sea.

Deliberately they made the paths of gravel so that plants could self-seed, and *Osteospermum* 'Langtrees' was the happy result. Thought to have *Osteospermum* 'Speckled' as one parent, this low-growing form bears a succession of purple-pink flowers all through the summer. It is hardier than most, although as the garden seldom suffered frost this quality was not severely tested at Langtrees.

Both Rogersons were plant enthusiasts, and were soon be-friended by great gardeners in the area, such as Margery Fish and Norman Hadden (*qv*), who were generous with advice, encourage-ment and many plants for the new garden. Finding things to give such formidable plantsmen in return posed something of a problem. On one occasion, learning that Norman Hadden badly wanted a guppy for his tropical fish tank, the Rogersons acquired one and with care and trepidation transported it in a jam jar. When they arrived it was to discover that the fish had produced babies on the way, so a delighted Norman Hadden received not one but seven guppys. After bad winters the Rogersons were often able to return to various owners plants that had been lost in the harsher conditions inland, and this helped to balance the equation.

The flow of plants was not all one way either. They enjoyed going off on plant hunting holidays to places such as Mount Kenya and the Picos Mountains of Spain, bringing back bulbs and seeds to share; they also visited gardens and nurseries in different parts of this country.

In one small nursery on the outskirts of Manchester they were delighted to find a particularly appealing dicentra, which had finely-cut glaucous leaves, beautifully offsetting the arched sprays of white flowers, each with just a hint of pink. The plant has proved to be a real gem, tolerant of most conditions including dry shade, and flowering for months on end. Its parentage has been much argued about, some authorities regarding it as a hybrid, with *Dicentra formosa oregana* as a parent, others concluding that it is just a good white form of *Dicentra formosa*. There is also little to choose between *D*. 'Langtrees' and *D*. 'Pearl Drops', a seedling produced by Alan Bloom of Bressingham. The Manchester nursery could shed no light on the question, for when the Rogersons returned some time later it had become a building site.

Tony Rogerson was colour blind, and therefore particularly appreciated plants with silver or variegated leaves. From the same nursery he came away with a *Brunnera macrophylla* which had small silvery dots along its leaves. It makes a good groundcover plant, tolerating more sun than the fully variegated form, which tends to scorch. A piece of this spotted plant was given to Margery Fish, who in time sold it as *Brunnera* 'Aluminium Spot'. Graham Thomas however named it *B. macrophylla* 'Langtrees', and it is under that name that it is most commonly known.

As a country doctor Dr Rogerson made frequent home visits to patients, and often returned with interesting plants and cuttings from their gardens. It is thought that one of them was the dark form of *Francoa sonchifolia* now called 'Rogerson's Form'. The delicate wands of flowers on 18in (45cm) stems are a particularly dark pink, although unfortunately no hardier than the type.

In 1976 the Rogersons left Langtrees and spent ten years in America before returning to Britain, where sadly Dr Rogerson died in 1987.

DR MOLLY SANDERSON

Viola 'Molly Sanderson'

Not many modern cultivars can have become fixed in gardeners' affections as fast as *Viola* 'Molly Sanderson'. This distinctive viola has the characteristics of a real classic, but quite how it came about is a mystery.

Dr Molly Sanderson lives in Northern Ireland, where in the 1950's she began to be fascinated by plants and gardening. A talk by Will Ingwersen, given at an Alpine Garden Society meeting, sparked off an enthusiasm for alpine plants, but her interests soon broadened to include other aspects of gardening. 'My gardening career has been a succession of love affairs with different genera', she says, primroses, rhododendron, mertensia, viola, hepatica, geranium, eryngium and hosta having all been particular passions over the years.

At Margate in Kent lived Scott Stone, another doctor who was an enthusiastic plantsman. In the 1970's when Molly Sanderson and her husband happened to be in the area, they called to see his half-acre garden, which was packed with rare and interesting things. A friendship was struck up and the following year he visited them in Ireland, bringing various plant offerings. Amongst these was a small viola simply labelled *'Viola niger'*, which was duly planted in the Sanderson's garden.

The new viola proved so vigorous and easy to propagate that Molly Sanderson tried it in several places, finding that it did best in a south-facing raised bed, where there was plenty of moisture. There the viola spread into a broad clump, producing its strangely matt, almost black flowers in succession from Spring until late Autumn. It was still flowering in late November of 1983 when Ralph Haywood of Wisley visited the Sanderson's garden. 'Not only did I see plants that I had only read about', he later reported enthusiastically, 'but many of them were still giving a good account of themselves'. He was intrigued by the viola, describing the colour as 'the nearest thing to black I have seen in a flower', and returned to Wisley with cuttings.

Dr Stone had died, so could shed no light on how the plant had been obtained, but enquiries were made, and Haywood consulted viola growers as to the plant's likely origin. Three years later he concluded, 'although its parentage is uncertain, my research suggests it is *Viola tricolor* crossed with a "pansy" type'. The plant was known to gardeners, it seemed, but under several different names, such as 'Black Knight', 'All Black' and 'Penny Black', but none of these names had been validly published or registered. '*Viola niger*' could not be used officially, since Latin names may not be given to modern cultivars. Ralph Haywood had researched the plant thoroughly, however, and there was now a specimen in the Wisley Herbarium and official description of it as *Viola* 'Molly Sanderson'. Several nurseries were listing it as such, and to bring order out of chaos he believed the name should stay.

Feeling that this situation was not altogether just, Dr Sanderson contacted Dr Stone's widow, who was sure he would not have minded. Thus, this good-tempered and endearing little plant has remained as *Viola* 'Molly Sanderson', becoming more widely-known with every year. It continues to grow in its namesake's garden, but there the label alongside still says firmly, '*Viola niger*'.

SHADOWS

Mrs Oakley Fisher

Rose 'Mrs Oakley Fisher'

This is a beautiful rose, with bronzy foliage and large, single flowers, of a rich and subtle orangey-yellow. It has a good scent, and all these elements, plus a name that has overtones of Beatrix Potter, make one wonder who Mrs Oakley Fisher was.

The rose was launched by the famous rose breeders, Cants of Colchester in 1921. 'As a rose for table decoration it will hold its own with any variety of its class', they declared, 'and is certainly distinct from all'. They were right, for the rose is still a favourite, seventy years on.

Mrs Oakley Fisher is believed to have been a friend of one of the Cant family, and married to a parson. Crockfords Directory reveals that there was a family named Oakley who, father and son, were Rectors of various parishes in the area, but no Oakley Fishers appear. A trawl through the Registers of Births, Marriages and Deaths at St Catherine's House in London has likewise yielded no-one of that name, so the lady remains an enigma.

Dr Jamain

Rose 'Souvenir du Dr Jamain'

This superb, dark red, Hybrid Perpetual rose was bred by Monsieur Francois Lacharme of Lyons, in 1865, but owes the resurgence of its popularity in the twentieth century to Vita Sackville-West. She found this neglected rose in a Sussex nursery, grew it at Sissinghurst, and gave cuttings away. Its velvety, wine-coloured flowers have a wonderful scent, and it would be satisfying to know whom the flower commemorated. Enquiries, however, only throw up a host of Jamains.

A French-bred rose named 'Madame Ferdinand Jamain', was launched in 1875, there was also a rose named 'Madame Hippolyte Jamain', and another called 'Paul Jamain'. There was a rose breeder called Dupuy Jamain, whose name is often spelt 'Jamin', and another Paris nursery named Messrs Jamin et Durand which sold fruit trees and roses.

Probably none of these Jamains have any link with the eponymous Dr Jamain. It is reasonable to suppose that he was a friend or customer of Monsieur Lacharme's and therefore likely to have lived near Lyons, and that he died in the 1860's.

Mrs Kendal Clark

Geranium 'Mrs Kendal Clark'

Like 'Mrs Oakley Fisher', 'Mrs Kendal Clark' trips off the tongue nicely, and is also the name of a very good plant. *Geranium* 'Mrs Kendal Clark' is a form of our native *Geranium pratense*, but produces pale blue flowers, faintly streaked with white. Surprisingly, it comes true from seed, and has held its own as a choice border plant for nearly sixty years.

It was sent to Walter Ingwersen of Birch Farm Nursery in the 1930's by Mrs Kendal Clark, and he offered it for sale about 1938. Walter Ingwersen had a wide circle of gardening friends, and probably this discerning lady was one. Unfortunately, who she was, and how she came by this distinctive plant, he never recorded, and she seems to have left no other trace.

Madame Isaac Pereire

Rose 'Madame Isaac Pereire'

Mark Fenwick of Abbotswood (*qv*) once said of 'Madame Isaac Pereire', 'I believe it is the loveliest and the latest, the largest and the sweetest rose in the garden'. 'Madame Isaac Periere' has certainly become one of the most widely-planted nineteenth century roses. It is said to have been named after the wife of a French banker, but about her nothing seems to have been written. Intriguingly, however, the flower began life under a quite different name.

It was the creation, about 1876, of a rose breeder named Garcon, who named his showy, long-flowering seedling 'Bienheureux de la Salle'. He appears later to have sold the rose to another specialist, Monsieur Jules Margottin, who exhibited it in London in 1884, but under the name of 'Madame Isaac Pereire'.

This caused the French magazine 'Journal des Roses', to drop dark hints about dirty tricks. It seems that the London Horticultural Society was in the habit of awarding prizes to the breeders of roses, rather than to the firm exhibiting them. By changing the name, Monsieur Margottin made it seem like a new introduction.

He probably did the rose a favour, however. The saying, 'A rose is a rose, is a rose', is all very well, but it is questionable whether even such a good rose as this would have won fame and affection as 'Bienheureux de la Salle'. Names do become part of a plant's personality.

SELECTED BIBLIOGRAPHY

Great Gardens of Britain, Peter Coats 1967
Shrub Roses of Today, Graham Stuart Thomas 1980
The Old Shrub Roses, Graham Stuart Thomas 1983
Climbing Roses Old and New, Graham Stuart Thomas 1983
History of the Rose, Roy E. Shepherd 1954
Companion to Roses, Fisher 1986
Dictionary of Roses, Millar Gault and Synge 1971
Roses, Pleasures and Treasures, Peter Coats 1962
Seven Gardens, E. B. Anderson 1973
Gardening on Chalk and Limestone, E. B. Anderson 1965
Heaths and Heathers, Terry L. Underhill 1971
English Heather Garden, Maswell and Patrick 1966
Daffodils, Tulips and Hardy Bulbs, M. J. Jefferson Brown 1966
The Daffodil, M. J. Jefferson Brown 1951
Modern Lilies, M. J. Jefferson Brown 1965
Garden Lilies, M. E. Leeburn 1963
Complete Book of Lilies, Rockwell, Grayson and De Graaf 1961
Lilies for Garden and Greenhouse, D. T. Macfie 1939
Lilies, Woodcock & Coutts 1936
Lilies and Their Cultivation, M. E. Leeburn 1955
Snowdrops and Snowflakes, Sir Frederick Stern 1956
The Gardener's Book of Trees, Allan Mitchell 1981
Conifers for Your Garden, Adrian Bloom 1972
Trees and Shrubs Hardy in the British Isles, W. J. Bean (revised
    Mitchell 1980)
Period Piece, Gwen Raverat 1952
Collecting Antique Plants, Roy Genders 1971
Ornamental Shrubs, C. E. Lucas Phillips and Peter Barber 1981
A Garden of Memories, Collingwood Ingram 1970
The Magic Tree, NCCPG Devon Group 1989
My Garden in Spring, E. A. Bowles 1914
My Garden in Summer, E. A. Bowles 1914
My Garden in Autumn and Winter, E. A. Bowles 1914
E. A. Bowles and His Garden, Mea Allan 1973
Manual of Cultivated Broadleaved Trees and Shrubs, G. Krussman
    1984
The English Flower Garden, William Robinson 1883
The Wild Garden, William Robinson 1870
Clematis, Christopher Lloyd 1977
Clematis, Ernest Markham 1935

William Robinson, Mea Allan 1982
Growing Hardy Perennials, Kenneth Beckett 1981
Hillier's Manual of Trees and Shrubs 1984
Better Gardening, R. Lane Fox 1982
The Classic Horticulturalist, Buchan and Colborn 1987
An Irish Flower Garden, Nelson and Walsh 1984
Hidcote, The Making of a Garden, Ethne Clark 1989
Eminent Gardeners, Jane Brown 1990
Perennial Garden Plants, Graham Stuart Thomas 1982
Scented Flora of the World, R. Genders 1977
A Chalk Garden, Sir Frederick Stern 1960
Fisons Guide to Gardens, Mea Allan 1970
English Gardens, Edward Hyams 1964
Magnolias and Camellias, Douglas Bartrum 1959
Garden Variety, Sir Arthur Hort 1935
Gardener's Encyclopaedia of Plants and Flowers, Brickell 1989
The Mill Garden, A. T. Johnson 1949
Geraniums, Peter Yeo 1985
Rhododendrons and Magnolias, Douglas Bartum 1957
Letters from a Cornish Garden, C. C. Vyvyan 1972
Fuchsias, S. J. Wilson 1970
Growing Fuchsias, Jennings and Miller 1979
Fuchsia Lexicon, Ewart 1982
Fuchsias for House and Garden, Clapham 1982
Chimps, Champs and Elephants, Jack Baker 1988
Flowers and Their Histories, Alice Coats 1956
Effective Flowering Shrubs, M. Haworth-Booth 1962
A Dictionary of Shrubs, S. Millar-Gault 1976
In An Irish Garden, Connolly and Dillon 1986
An Architect of Nature, Luther Burbank 1939
The Harvest of the Years, Burbank and Hall 1927
Gardening and Beyond, Florence Bellis 1986
Plants from the Past, Stuart and Sutherland 1987
Irish Gardening and Horticulture, Nelson and Brady 1980
Constance Spry, E. Coxhead 1975
A Horticultural Who's Who, Simmonds 1948
The Makers of Heavenly Roses, J. Harkness 1985
Miss Willmott of Warley Place, A. Le Lievre 1980
Saxifrages of Europe, Webb and Gornell
The Damp Garden, Beth Chatto 1982
Clematis, the Queen of Climbers, J. M. Fisk 1976

Modern Rhododendrons, E. H. M. Cox and P. A. Cox 1955
A Century of Gardeners, B. Massingham 1982
The Genus Rosa, Ellen Willmott 1910–1914
British Gardeners, Hadfield, Harling and Lighton 1980
Dictionary of Gardening, Royal Horticultural Society 1956 (supplement 1969)
British and Irish Botanists and Horticulturists, Desmond 1977
Bibliography of British Gardens, Desmond 1984
The Plant Finder 1988, 1989, 1990, 1991

Periodicals
Journal of the Royal Horticultural Society 1846–
Journal of the Royal National Rose Society 1876–
Journal of Alpine Garden Society 1930–
Gardener's Chronicle 1841–
My Garden 1930–51
New Flora and Silva 1928–40
Hortus 1987–
The Plantsman 1979–

Index